Cecil J. Zuber
is a member of the
British Squash Professionals Association.
He is highly regarded
throughout the squash world
as a coach and player
and has won every major tournament
at the amateur, open, and club levels
in Singapore and Malaysia.

CECIL J. ZUBER

squash

for players and coaches

PRENTICE-HALL, INC. A SPECTRUM BOOK Englewood Cliffs, N.J. 07632

Library of Congress Cataloging in Publication Data

ZUBER, CECIL J.
    Squash for players and coaches.

    (A Spectrum Book)
    Revision of Squash rackets for coaches and
players originally published in 1977 by Australia
& New Zealand Book Co., Sydney.
    1. Squash rackets (Game)   I. Title.
GV1004.Z82 1980   796.34'3   80-15784
ISBN 0-13-839910-7
ISBN 0-13-839902-6 (pbk.)

Editorial/production supervison and interior design by Carol Smith
Manufacturing buyer: Barbara A. Frick

Originally published as *Squash Rackets for Coaches and Players*
by Australia & New Zealand Book Co Pty Ltd, Sydney, Australia.

© 1980 by Prentice-Hall, Inc., *Englewood Cliffs, New Jersey 07632*

A SPECTRUM BOOK

10 9 8 7 6 5 4 3 2 1

Printed in the United States of America

PRENTICE-HALL INTERNATIONAL, INC., *London*
PRENTICE-HALL OF AUSTRALIA PTY. LIMITED, *Sydney*
PRENTICE-HALL OF CANADA, LTD., *Toronto*
PRENTICE-HALL OF INDIA PRIVATE LIMITED, *New Delhi*
PRENTICE-HALL OF JAPAN, INC., *Tokyo*
PRENTICE-HALL OF SOUTHEAST ASIA PTE. LTD., *Singapore*
WHITEHALL BOOKS LIMITED, *Wellington, New Zealand*

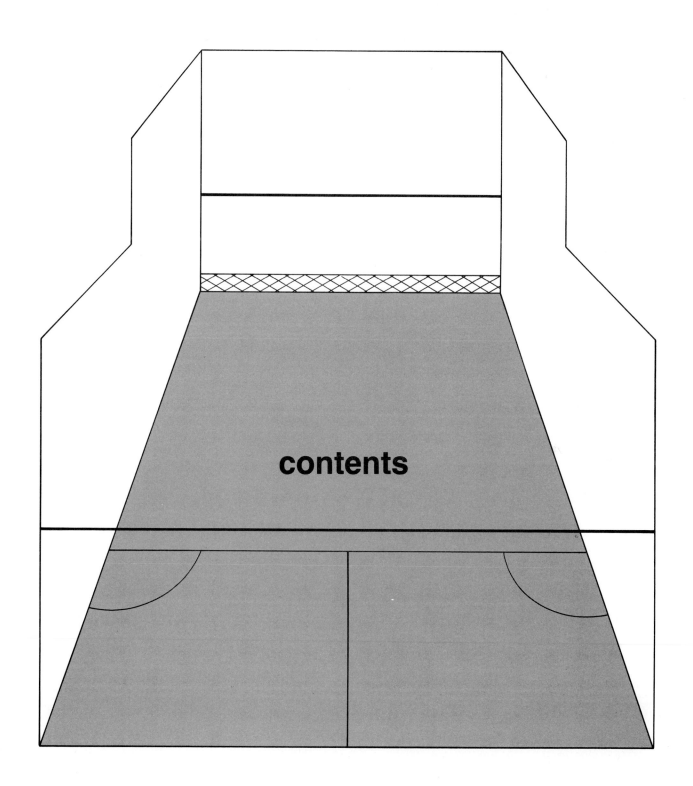

contents

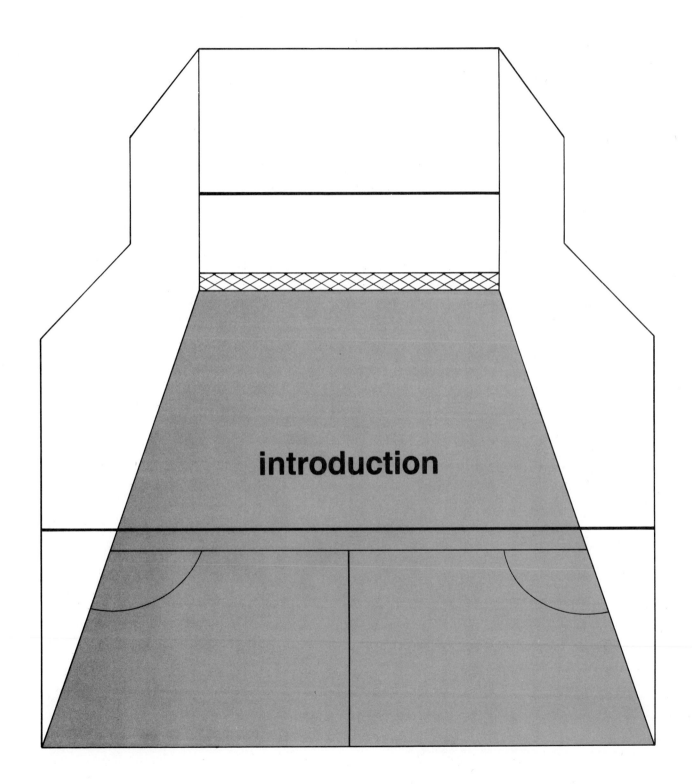

introduction

Squash is an easy game to play badly—it is a difficult game to play well.

Any two people, with a reasonable amount of ball sense, can walk onto a court for the first time, play a game, and derive both exercise and satisfaction from the experience.

The game currently is one of the world's fastest growing sports, having earned this popularity because of a number of factors. Unlike a game such as tennis where the ball must go over the net for the game to continue, the squash ball rebounds off the wall(s) for the opponent to return; it can be played in any weather or climatic condition, day or night; a great deal of exercise can be had in a short time; equipment is comparatively cheap; and a number of courts, even of multi-story construction, can be built on a small plot of land.

This continuing trend, with more and more people playing, contributes to the demand by top level players for that little bit extra in technical skill, physical fitness, or mental attitude to provide an edge over the opponent.

Although this book will be invaluable to advanced players, the chapters are designed in such a way that a raw beginner can learn to play the game from scratch and advance to championship level. Very little divides the top

ten professionals in the world today, as they all possess a high degree of technical skill, and are all able to play the full repertoire of shots. The difference is in playing the right shot, at the right time, when under physical and mental stress. This psychological aspect is of ever-increasing importance.

A separate chapter (Chapter 10) is devoted to advanced shots, not because they are new (there are no new shots in squash), but to show some of the replies which can be made from various situations, and, more importantly, to get the player to *think*.

Similarly, while Chapter 9 on the subject of advanced tactics provides a wealth of information that can help to win matches, it should once again stimulate the player to think more about the game, both on and off the court.

I have drawn upon my own knowledge, and the knowledge of those eminently qualified in the fields of physiology and sports medicine to highlight some of the aspects of the body's functions which are affected during a game of squash. These are discussed in Chapter 11, "Fitness Training," which is designed to help prepare the player both physically and psychologically.

"For the Veterans" (Chapter 12) has

been written especially for the player whose advancing years place him among the senior club members and tournament competitors. The senior member's game cannot help but undergo change as he ages, and the suggestions and tactics which are incorporated in this chapter will encourage him not only to continue to play, and play well, but to win tournaments.

The coaching and playing techniques described have been developed and tested over many years of hard experience, and I am confident that those who follow them will not only beat most people, but will become fitter, healthier, and will derive more satisfaction from the game, whether aiming for the top of the championship tree or merely playing for social enjoyment.

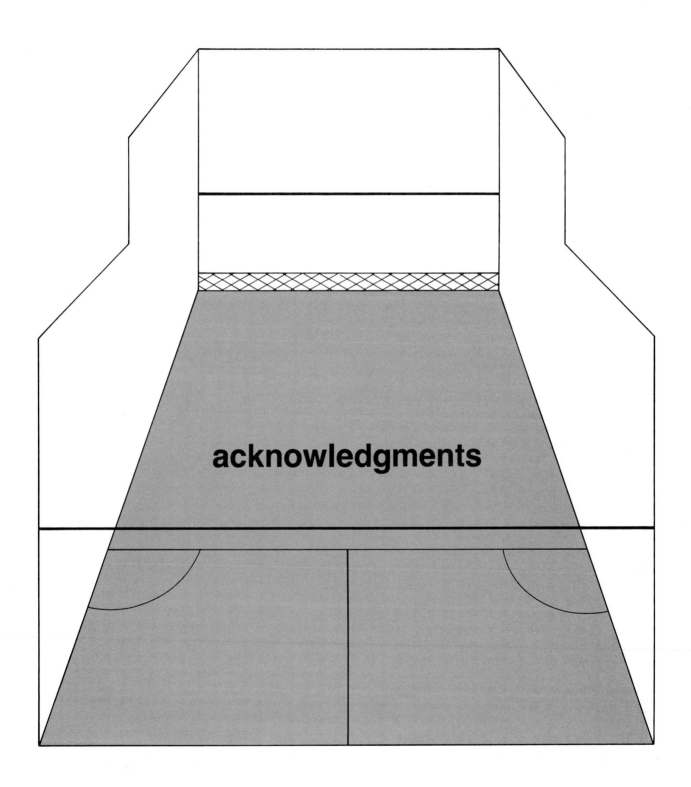

acknowledgments

To write a book of this nature would not be possible without the assistance of many people. In particular my indebtedness goes to Miss Lorraine Hoowarth for her excellent artwork and photography; Dr. Grahame Budd, Senior Lecturer in Environmental Health, and Miss Barbara McPhee, Physiotherapist, both from the School of Public Health and Tropical Medicine, The University of Sydney; Pakistan International Airlines Corporation for their help and the supply of photographs; likewise the Squash Rackets Association; Manly-Warringah squash courts, where many of the photographs were taken; Dunlop-Slazengers, who supplied equipment and clothing; those publishers who kindly gave permission for the use of selected passages from their books; my wife for her forbearance as a squash widow over these many years, and my three sons, worthy opponents, the eldest of whom appears with me in many of the photographs; and to those of the squash fraternity throughout the world who, as opponent and pupil alike, unknowingly enabled me to gain the knowledge and expertise necessary to make this book possible: Professor Per-Olof Astrand, *Health and Fitness* Skandia Insurance Company Limited, Stockholm, 1973; Professor Per-Olof Astrand & Kaarl Rodahl, *Textbook of Work Physiology*, McGraw-Hill Book Company, New York, 1970; Kenneth H. Cooper, *The New Aerobics*, Bantam Books Inc., New York, 1970; J. V. G. A. Durnin & R. Passmore, *Energy, Work and Leisure*, Heinemann Educational Books Ltd., London, 1967; the *Journal of the American Medical Association*; C. S. Leithead & A. R. Lind, *Heat Stress and Heat Disorders*, Cassell & Collier Macmillan Publishers Ltd., London, 1964; Dr. David C. Reid, the University of Alberta, Canada.

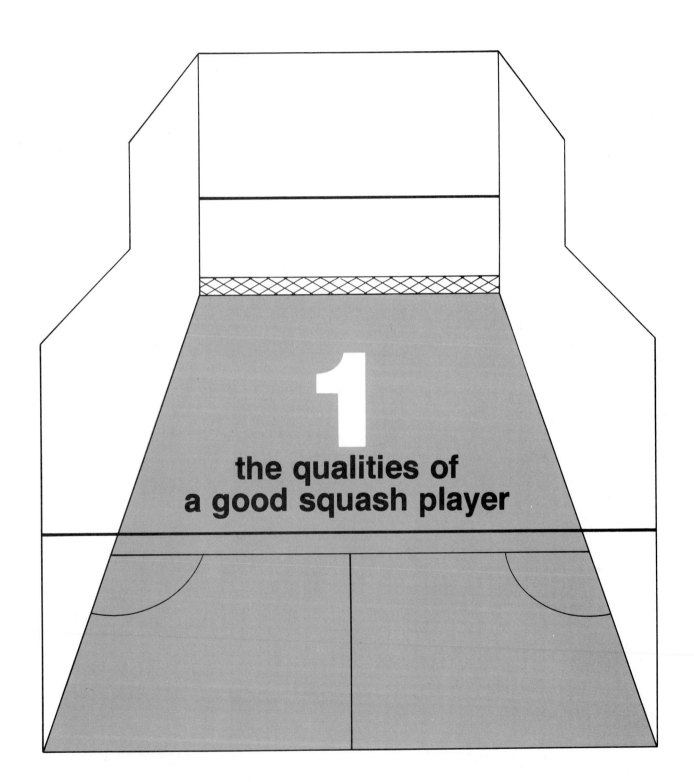

1
the qualities of a good squash player

THE QUALITIES

I have been asked many times what makes a good squash player. In degree of importance, I rank the necessary qualities as:

1. ball control and good stroke production

2. fitness and stamina

3. mobility

4. concentration

5. patience

6. tactical brain

7. dedication

8. experience

9. style.

Their Relative Importance

To be a good player one needs to possess all nine qualities. However, unless the ball can be controlled in every aspect, the other eight fade into insignificance, and all the fitness, or mobility, or any other attribute in the world will not win matches.

The prime concern of the coach must be to instill into the pupil the need to control the ball, for unless this is done it cannot be hit hard with any telling effect. Having reached the stage where they can hit the ball more often than not, most players are gripped with an incredible belief that the harder they hit the ball, the more chance they have of overwhelming their opponent. This could not be further from the truth.

Ball control, and fitness and stamina are ranked so highly that separate chapters (Chapters 4 and 11) have been devoted to these qualities in order to deal at length with the many aspects of each.

The assertion that one needs to possess all nine qualities to be a good player is valid, and will remain valid for as long as the game is played. All qualities must fit together like a jigsaw puzzle to ensure a complete package, for if only one part is missing, the player's game will fall apart. The difference between the good player and the champion is in expertise which is acquired, and application of these qualities by one player against the other. But for those who apply themselves to the task, there is no reason why championship level cannot be attained.

MOBILITY

Many different words could hve been used to describe this quality—words or expressions such as *speed, fleetness-of-foot, nimble-footed, rapidly covering ground, élan,* and many more. But none seems as appropriate as *mobility,* which, for the writer, embodies all of the movement, flexibility, and speed rolled into one word.

Mobility is a by-product of, and a direct result of the hard training which gives "tone" to the muscles of the legs—and as squash is a game of body and mind, it is the legs which have to get that body into the position to be able to play the shot.

Having been brought up in the Pakistani style of play, through my coach Mohamed Amin, I am ever mindful of the need for body flexibility.

Stance and Balance

The tendency among Westerners is to be too upright, uptight and rigid on the court, and this rigidity reduces the flexibility needed in the lower reaches. Never permit pupils to stand on the court wih their legs stiff. Their knees must be bent, and they must adopt a crouched stance, ready to spring in any direction, just like a cat. (See Figure 1.) There is a need to be able to start quickly, move with

FIGURE 1   Opponent's side-wall shot lands too short, but realizing this, he has remained crouched ready to move to my reply.

speed, stop abruptly, start again, change direction, spring, leap, bend, stretch, anticipate, and to retrieve that ball which appears to be impossible to reach. (See Figure 2.)

FIGURE 2   Both players are displaying fine anticipation, balance, and body flexibility.

When you reach the ball, you must be balanced, and in a position to play the shot of your choice, shot after shot, rally after rally. When watching top-level players one is sometimes staggered by the speed with which they retrieve the ball and the great sense of anticipation shown, but what one is seeing is the culmination of a lot of hard training. It has not been achieved by any easy means.

Timing the Stroke

A fault commonly found among players, and more particularly those who are fit and mobile, is that they move quickly to the ball, but then proceed to rush the stroke. The initial movement should be by way of long strides, short steps being used to adjust the feet and body into the correctly balanced position prior to striking the ball. It is the final few short steps that will determine the direction, placement and speed of the return, for before reaching this point the player will have made up his mind as to what shot he wants to play. A slight adjustment to stance and body movement can make all the difference between an attacking or defensive movement.

4

A rushed stroke under these circumstances invariably results in the player having a cramped body- and arm-movement, which results in subsequent loss of ball control. To counteract this, the player is taught to get to the ball quickly, then if at all possible, to stop and strike the ball as it is suspended in the air.

Keeping the Ball at a Distance

Playing the ball close to the body and *masking* the shot from an opponent will be discussed later, but for the moment, the importance is stressed of making a stroke with the ball away from the body, allowing freedom of movement and free flow of the shot. The tendency, except for advanced players, is to *crowd* most shots, a result of the striker failing to realize that the ball is closer than he thinks. At full stretch the distance from the shoulder to the end of the racket is about forty-four inches for the average man, and when the length of the rest of the body is added to this he has a lot of distance at his command. So, keep away from the ball.

If distance has been misjudged, it is easier—and affords better balance and ball control—to reach an extra couple of inches to make the stroke than to adjust back the same distance. For smoothness of play, for balance, and because of the need to get back into position for an opponent's return, the player leans into the ball at all times, even when hitting off the wrong foot.

Hitting the Early Ball

The player will be confronted constantly with split-second decision making, so must be capable of coming up with the right answer and ensuring its successful implementation. I am a great believer in taking the ball as early as possible, but to do this one must possess fleetness of foot, mobility, and balance. By taking an early ball you are denying your opponent the luxury of longer ball travel, hence time. For example, if you took a low volley on the *short line* as against on the first bounce, you have gained, let us say, twelve feet of travel (six feet each way) and one second of time. You have, therefore, effectively speeded up the game without having hit the ball any harder; forced your opponent to move faster, react faster, and possibly rush a shot; and denied him the chance to attack.

By taking the early ball your return may not be as good as you would like, but the advantages must be weighed against the disadvantages which result from such action. Remember: "It is better to hit a poor shot that goes 'up' than a good shot that goes 'down.'" (See Figure 1.) Once the ball hits the front wall your opponent is faced with a problem—he has to hit it; but if your "winner" goes down he doesn't have any problem—he has won the rally, or to be more correct, you have lost it.

Champions have the ability to hit the right shot at the right time, and this is what sets them apart from the average tournament player.

CONCENTRATION

Concentration, or lack of it, during a game can mean the difference between winning or losing. (See Figure 3.) However the thinking process should begin long before a player goes on to the court. You must think about the plan of play you intend to adopt, the tactics you intend to employ, how you can counter your opponent's strengths, and how to exploit his weaknesses.

Once on the court, it is essential that you think continuously, focusing all of your attentive powers. You must be constantly aware of your opponent's position, for this can have a bearing on your next shot. All too often do players hit the ball back to their opponent when, with thought and concentration, they could have played it to the opposite corner. Be positive in the thinking process as well as in stroke production, and if you have worked your opponent into a position where the winning shot is available, keep this advantage.

The Service

Concentrate on the service, for here at the start of the rally you hold every advantage. Maintain the advantage and do not be like so

FIGURE 3   Concentration of the highest order. My friends, and sometimes opponents, Ken Hiscoe (right) and Dick Carter in what I regard as the finest action photo ever taken. (Henderson Club, Auckland, N.Z., 1968.) More than any other Australians these two players are responsible for projecting their country into world squash. In 1962 they became the first Australians to compete in the British Amateur Championship with Hiscoe, beating T. Shafik (U.A.R.) in the final. Carter was a beaten finalist in 1965 and 1966, both matches being memorable 5 games.

many players who simply amble into the box, hit the ball while still strolling, and hope that it lands in the opponent's court. *Think* of what you are doing. Concentrate on where you want the ball to hit on the front wall, and eventually land. Be deliberate with the service—its delivery, speed, direction, and placement.

The Score
Concentrate on the score. As each game reaches a conclusion, a lost point at 6 to the opponent could be vital as it could be too late for you to catch up. It is easier to get back into the game early on when one may experience a lapse in concentration and have time to take corrective action.

Maintaining Concentration
The longer a game progresses, the more one tires mentally as well as physically. Concentration flags and a greater conscious effort has to be made to maintain this discipline. Mental alertness must be sustained and the ball watched a little closer.

When playing a left-hander be conscious of this fact, and change your game to play to his weaknesses—possibly his backhand, which is on your forehand side. And don't come off the court after losing the game expressing surprise when told that you had played a left-hander and didn't realize it. Concentrate on *everything* and develop an enquiring and inquisitive mind.

PATIENCE

Probably more than any other quality does that of patience highlight how all nine are dovetailed to provide a complete package—essential if one is to be a good squash player. Patience, fitness, and stamina go hand in hand. At the top level of championship play there may be seen many rallies of over a hundred or more shots, mostly drives up and down the wall or defensive lobs, for each player knows that his opponent has the speed, anticipation, and the power to retrieve almost anything, as well as a complete repertoire of shots.

Because of these factors, each finds it a risk to attempt a winner by hitting the ball just

6

above the tin, unless the right opportunity presents itself. The risks are far too great. Percentage squash is played with the accent on keeping the ball in play at all costs, allowing the opponent to make the mistakes. The patient, waiting game cannot be practiced unless one is fit. If one's fitness is suspect then one is forced to go for winners more often than is advisable.

So get fit, be patient, and be in no hurry to win. Give your opponent every opportunity to lose.

TACTICAL BRAIN

Although this quality appears in sixth position on the list, it is sufficiently important to warrant a separate chapter (Chapter 9) to put into perspective some of the various tactics that will increase the odds on you winning.

DEDICATION

Of the top ten players in the world at the time of writing, places 2, 3, 4, 5, and 10 are filled by Pakistanis; but Pakistan's debut in world squash was, if almost hesitant, certainly dramatic. The legendary Hashim Khan, serving with the Peshawar Club of Officers, was sent to compete in the British Open in 1950. Although age thirty-four at the time, he did what would have been thought almost incredible. He beat the Egyptian, Mahmoud Karim, in straight games, ending his three-year hold on the championship; and tributes were paid to his artistry as well as to the wonderful agility exhibited at an age which marks the beginning of the end for most players.

But why should the Pakistanis be so good? Admittedly there is a steady stream of outstanding players flowing from the PIA Squash Coaching Centre (the game now rivals hockey as the national sport), but bolstering fine coaching and the benefit of the experience of their predecessors, is the one quality which I believe points to their success—dedication. Their dedication to the game is complete, extending beyond the players to the administrators.

An example of the total involvement is the PIA Squash Complex in Karachi, which must rank as the most modern in the world, and certainly deserves the title, "The Home of Pakistan Squash." (See Figures 4 and 5.) The building consists of five glass-back-walled courts, eating areas, foyers, viewing spaces, a lounge, changing rooms, and external landscaped terraces. Two of the courts have seating facilities. One seats around 250 people with an additional spectators' gallery for 100 persons, and has provision for television coverage. The second championship court seats 150 spectators. Truly an impressive, exciting, and very functional squash facility.

EXPERIENCE

Like some of the other qualities that go to make a good squash player, there is no easy road or shortcut to experience. One may start playing the game possessing fitness, stamina, mobility, and patience, having the ability to concentrate, and be dedicated enough to apply oneself wholly to learning the game, but experience can only come with the passage of time.

How Long Does It Take

How long it takes to gain experience is up to each individual—whether he benefits from each game played; the number of tournaments entered; the competition available; and his own application to the learning process. The experience and expertise of one player can really only be assessed relative to that possessed by another—the champion of one club, or country, may seem quite mediocre in comparison with his opposite number somewhere else.

It takes time, and the results of many games played against a wide variety of opponents, before a store of knowledge can be built up—before one can be considered to be *experienced*. However, it is well to remember that nobody knows it all—there is something to be learned every time you play.

FIGURE 4   PIA Squash Complex, Karachi.

FIGURE 5   PIA Squash Complex, Karachi. Inside view of the championship court.

I was recently approached by a young man who said that he wanted some coaching. He told me that he had been playing for about six months, and in reply to my question as to what problems he thought he had, he replied that he wasn't having any trouble but that he felt his game needed "polishing up a bit." Before he hit the first ball I noticed that his grip was wrong and I told him so. This episode illustrates that not only was he inexperienced but that he didn't even have enough experience to know that, in fact, he knew very little.

Experience through Competition

You should play against as many different types of players as possible, at a level comparable to your own—some a little better, some not quite so good—and see how their particular style suits yours, or whether it has an upsetting and spoiling effect. When you think the time is right, enter club tournaments as both an individual and a team member, gradually upgrading your level.

Take the opportunity to compete in other championships and so widen your experience of the competitive styles that you will encounter. At first you may get beaten more often than you win, but this should not be a discouragement. Rather it should be considered as part and parcel of the growing-up process in the squash world, and a way of storing more and more knowledge of the game.

Learn from mistakes and defeats. In fact, sometimes more is to be learned from losing than winning, even if a loss is to a much better player. However, not only will the match be lost, but the opportunity to learn will be thrown away if you have not endeavored to learn from the experience.

STYLE

This quality, last on the list, is in its correct place. Style, like beauty, is in the eye of the beholder, and is very difficult to determine. What looks poor to one may draw rapt praise from another, but the generally accepted view of *good style* is the free-flowing movement of the body, with the racket swung in classical rythmic manner.

Style is, therefore, not everything, and probably the best example I can give is my early tutor, Hashim Khan. His grip is unorthodox; he is not what the purists call a *classic player*, but when he moves to, and plays the ball, the atmosphere for the spectators is electric. A style all his own, but how effective!

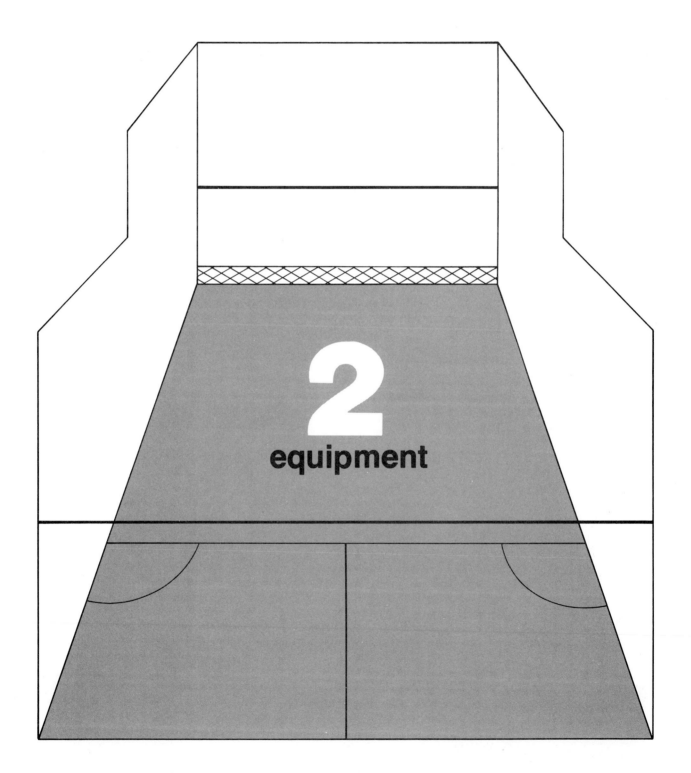

2
equipment

RACKET

There is a wide range of rackets on the market with an equally wide range of prices. I am of the opinion that a player must have the finest equipment if he is to give of his best in any sport. It is false economy to buy a cheap racket, as the one of good quality is made from finer material, is better balanced, and will stand up to a lot harder play—including the occasional bang on the wall or floor.

There is very little difference in the weight of rackets; they are all light, but balance does vary. So having chosen one of good quality that suits you, stick with it, as you will find that your *touch* and accuracy will become dependent upon *your* racket. I have used the same brand for many years simply because I consider it the best in every respect. The racket I use must have balance, *feel* and flexibility; and these qualities can only be found in a completely wooden frame. Do not choose one that has steel or some other material in the shaft, for such a racket is too rigid and is more liable to have the head break off if the wall or floor is struck. Not only is this expensive but it can be a danger to an opponent or spectator.

The grip will be either towelling or leather, and the one you choose will be purely a matter of preference. From experience I find that leather provides a better grip under all conditions for longer periods, whereas the towelling becomes greasy and/or hard, requiring constant replacement.

Players are advised, even when playing in colder climates, to wear a towelling wrist band. This prevents sweat from running down the arm and into the hand. A wet hand results in a loose grip, affects stroke making, and faces the player with the possibility of the racket slipping completely out of the hand.

STRINGS

Having chosen your racket(s) wisely, you must consider the strings. Once again what you are looking for is feel, and this can only come from natural gut—not from nylon or synthetic materials. Unless you are in the championship class, or at an advanced level, you will probably own only one racket so will want strings that give this feel but are durable as well. Your choice should be a comparatively thick gauge of gut.

My rackets are strung with either fine or

thick gauge depending upon the use to which I put them. Those I use for tournament play are strung with a fine gauge as I need this for accuracy. However, being fine, the strings fray quickly and need to be replaced more often. My everyday and practice rackets have a thicker gauge, and like those I use in championship play, are strung tightly. Your racket, like mine, should be tightly strung, as this allows the strings to do a lot of the work for you in stroke production, and propels the ball faster, with greater accuracy.

BALL

In squash there are basically two types of balls: the English or international ball, and the American ball. The difference between the two is that the American ball is harder and faster than the English ball. A seeming anomaly of squash is that the slower the ball the faster the game, so the English game is considered the faster of the two. The official ball for American tournaments is the 70-plus white-dot ball, while the English yellow-dot ball is the approved ball for international competition.

CLOTHING

Traditionally, and by order of rule no. 25 of the rules approved by the International Squash Rackets Federation, "Players are required to wear white clothing." However, with the increasing amount of time being allotted to the game on TV, pastel colored clothing is coming more into vogue. There should be no strong objection to this, but too dark a color can be not only distracting but can cause the ball to occasionally get lost in this dark background.

The shirt and shorts should allow for freedom of movement and be absorbent, as you will sweat, at times quite profusely. In the tropics, many players prefer to use shorts made of a lightweight cotton, and a lightweight Chinese cotton T-shirt. These clothes absorb the sweat but, being light to start with, do not become too heavy—and an encumbrance—when saturated. The shirt is always changed after every game. In a cold climate one does not sweat as much, and it is always a good idea to have a sweater on during the hit-up, and to put back on after the game rather than stand around getting cold before taking a shower.

SOCKS

Your feet will have to do a lot of running in the course of a match so don't torture them with cheap, ill-fitting socks. Buy a good quality pair(s), wool for preference, which are able to absorb the sweat, and have a cushion sole. The socks should fit properly, being neither too large nor too small, allowing room for the toes to move.

SHOES

Many good quality shoes are sold in the marketplace and the choice is yours, but be careful in your selection and choose a pair that has a nonmarking sole, provides support, has a good grip, is flexible, and not heavy. Also ensure that they are light in weight, for there is going to be a lot of strain put upon the muscles of the leg. Don't put further strain on the legs by carrying more weight on the feet than is necessary.

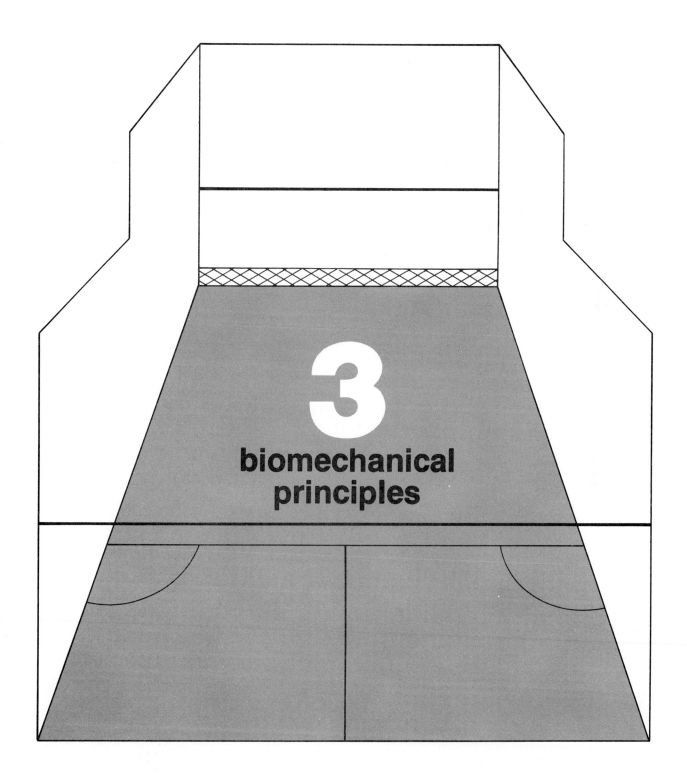

3
biomechanical
principles

BASIC PRINCIPLES

With squash blooming in popularity throughout the world, the demand has increased for coaching; unfortunately all too often it is found that coaches do not, or are unable to, effectively pass on their knowledge to either the beginner or advanced player. A good coach will have an enquiring, analytical and inquisitive mind, and be capable of getting the player to think of why he does everything on the squash court, from hitting the ball, to where and how coordination of body movement relates to ball control and direction.

It is quite pointless to teach squash in a mechanical fashion. It must be explained to the player why he should perform in a certain way. He should be conditioned to analyzing his performance in all aspects of the game with the four questioning words: *Why?, Where?, When?, How?*. If he does not, the learning curve will flatten rapidly.

The basic principles of the game must be taught, and for the beginner no allowance for variation, for unless he learns the correct methods he will be unable to adapt to minor changes in physical strength, body shape, weight and size, natural movement patterns, etc. Because of the speed of the game, the player cannot always be in the correct position and make the classical stroke, but unless he has learned correctly from the outset he will have difficulty in playing when under pressure, possibly off-balance, and on the wrong foot.

COORDINATION OF MIND AND BODY

The player will need to know the correct grip; when and how to move his feet, and bend the knees and body; and how to watch the ball. In other words, he must exercise complete coordination of mind and body. But to have true and effective meaning for the pupil, the instruction should be explicit. Example by demonstration is an excellent medium for transmission of information, as against such often-heard comments by the coach as: "You didn't get your foot across," or "You hit the ball too early." A demonstration of what should be done, followed by what the pupil actually did, makes the differences manifest, and is more likely to have lasting beneficial effect.

SELECTING OPPONENTS
FOR PRACTICE

Players should be encouraged to play against two categories of opponents—those they can beat without too much difficulty, and those they cannot. The difference in standards should not be too great, for the whole exercise would be abortive if a player of medium standard chose an outright beginner at one end of the spectrum and a champion at the other. By playing an inferior opponent, the player can put into practice what he has learned and will be able to attack the ball, but against a superior opponent he is under pressure and, being forced to defend more often, will not have time in many rallies to play the shot he would like.

COACHING METHODS

Once players have progressed beyond the raw beginner stage and are capable of playing a range of shots, coaching sessions should take the form of a game during which the coach advises the pupil to play the shot he considers appropriate during the rally. The coach can explain why he or the pupil hit such-and-such a winner, and comment on some of the *shots* played, or how it was possible for the pupil to make a winner, and why—always *Why?*.

This method is a useful form of instruction, for the demonstration and explanation immediately follow the action. As a form of "instant replay" the coach should explain where the pupil went wrong and what shot he should have played for maximum penetration of an opponent's weakness, and should then try to recreate the same situation in the next rally. A good coach will adjust the level of his play to just above that of his pupil, and will hit winners as a form of demonstration only. Nothing whatsoever is achieved by a coach who plays winners to bolster his ego or impress any spectators who may be present; but he has done his job well if the pupil progresses to the stage where he beats the master.

A player's weakness(es) must be analyzed, but before taking corrective action the coach should explain where the weakness is, how it has developed, and why. Such weaknesses as there may be could have crept into a player's game quite simply because he has the wrong grip, the incorrect stance or swing, or because of any number of seemingly insignificant factors that are visible only to an observant coach.

THE MOST DIFFICULT SHOT

All players have a weakness, or are weaker in some part of their game, and while the coach must aim to alleviate any problem area, the player himself must identify any such weakness and try to mask that facet of his game when playing. It is recognised by most leading players that the hardest shot of the lot is the high ball on the backhand, for here the arm is extended, allowing of very little effective control. Accepting this as a difficult shot, the player conditions himself to defending at this time, with as good a return as possible, being content to attack later. As a coach you have a responsibility to your pupil in particular and to the game in general, and should never confuse the player with complex explanations. Be simple, to the point, explicit, and always make common sense.

GRIP

The speed of the game coupled with the need for fast reflex action does not allow time (nor is it desirable) to change the grip for backhand and forehand. One grip must be used throughout. One hears of minor variations to the *orthodox* grip but this is not advocated, for as we will see later, it is not possible to develop a *sliced* stroke effectively unless, with the racket held correctly, the ball is hit *flat*.

Shake Hands with the Racket

The correct grip is obtained by holding the head of the racket vertical and shaking hands with the handle (as shown in Figures 6, 7, and 8). Naturally the grip must feel comfortable, the racket being gripped near the end of the handle or a little further up. How-

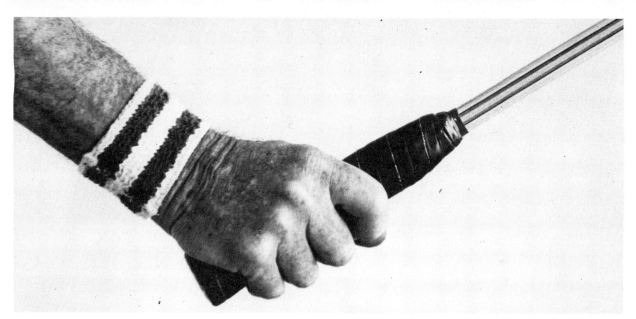

FIGURE 6   Correct grip, from outside the hand.

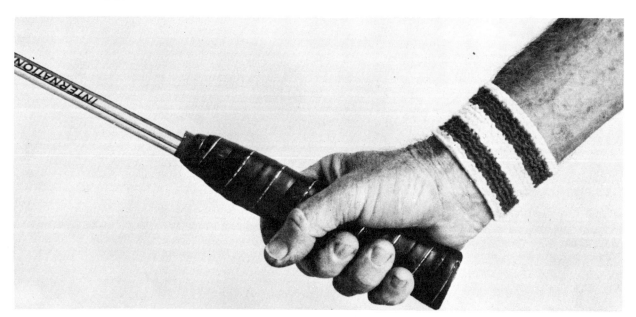

FIGURE 7   Correct grip, from inside the hand.

FIGURE 8   Correct grip, from above.

ever, irrespective of the distance from the end, the position of the hand in relation to racket head does not change. The fingers should be slightly spread with the space between the forefinger and second finger a little extended to assist control. The thumb grips the handle in a manner similar to holding a hammer when knocking in a nail. (See Figures 6, 7, and 8.) There is a tendency among beginners to extend the thumb along the handle in the mistaken belief that they will obtain greater control. The reverse is true. It is sometimes found that a player will extend the forefinger along the handle for the same reason, with the same ineffective result. With the racket held in the correct grip, the outside edge of the racket head, when held vertically, will project a line down the shaft and into the V formed by the thumb and forefinger. A slight turning of the grip from the vertical will be easily spotted by the coach, as the stroke will appear cramped and uneven, and depending upon the degree of incorrectness in the grip, the ball will travel too high or too low.

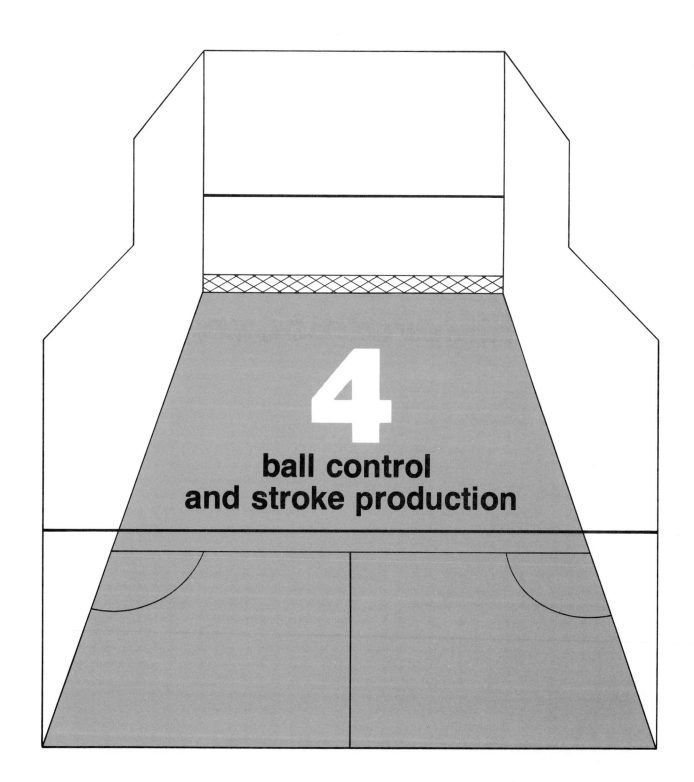

4
ball control and stroke production

INTRODUCTION

The service has been made and the rally begins. The receiver of the serve faces the first problem, and from then on uses every resource at his command to solve or create further problems. Upon how he and his opponent cope will depend the outcome of each rally—and the match. Squash should be thought of in the simplest of terms, with the player coming down to the basics of the game, for only if the essentials and correct methods are understood and employed, is it possible to develop to a good standard of play and reach championship level.

There are players who never intend to play other than socially, but more enjoyment and playing satisfaction will come their way if they improve steadily, and win more often than they lose. The urge to win is in most of us. Ground strokes constitute the bread-and-butter of the game, those that comprise the rest of the repertoire at the champion's command being the *topping*.

How to Win by Not Losing

As stated earlier, a player need know only the service and one other shot to win—or to be more correct, to not lose—more often than not. The secret is ball control. If the player has this command over the ball, and is able to place it where he wants, at the speed he wishes, he is allowing his opponent every opportunity to make errors.

Good players possess this ability, which is considered the most important on the list of qualities discussed in the first chapter. However, to put the above plan of action into practice he must possess the additional qualities of fitness and stamina, mobility, concentration, and patience. For the moment, let us put aside those other qualities and return to them later.

The one shot (in addition to the service) under consideration is one hit to a length down the side wall, which keeps the opponent pinned in the back corner(s). (For the purpose of this discussion, the backhand and/or forehand are accepted as being one shot.) It will readily become apparent that, for this plan to be successful, the player must, in addition to having mastered ball control, possess the four additional qualities referred to above, each being dependent upon the other. If only one link in the chain is missing, winning becomes more difficult. The player has to exercise *patience*, giving his opponent opportunities for making mistakes; but one cannot afford the luxury of patience if one's own *fitness and stamina* are suspect. And if fitness and stamina are lacking so is *mobility*, and certainly *concentration*, which must fade as fatigue sets in.

Play to a Length

The success or failure of this plan depends upon the ball being played to a length, i.e. to bounce for the second time in the back corner. This is not to imply that the ball must be hit hard, for the same result can be achieved from a slower return, which at times is advisable.

Various factors such as climatic conditions, speed of the court, ball speed, condition of wall and floor surface, etc. will have a bearing, out, in the main, the height above the tin where you hit the ball will determine the speed required to achieve a *length* on the return. Naturally a ball hit hard and high is more likely to present your opponent with a volley or an easy return off the back wall. Similarly, a lower and slower ball is likely to present him with a possible winner somewhere around the *short* line. A good general rule to follow is: "Low and hard; high and slow."

Back Corner Problem

As stated above, the ball should be played to a length to the back corner. However, it is not good enough to play to a length only to find the ball some distance out from the side wall, as this shot presents your opponent with an excellent chance to try a winner, or at least go into attack.

By keeping him in the back corner, you are forcing him to defend, and by playing the ball close to the side wall you have compounded his problem, rendering him more likely to make a mistake. At all times give your opponent the ball with a *lot of wall* near it rather than a ball surrounded by a *lot of air*.

Summary of Essentials
- Control the ball.
- Play to a length into the back corners.

- Give the ball *lots of wall* and *little air*.
- Hit hard—return low.
- Hit soft—return high.
- Keep your eye on the ball.
- Watch your opponent.
- Move to the *T* after every return.
- Be patient.
- Don't go for the winner on every shot.
- Give your opponent the opportunity to make a mistake.

BALL-CONTROL DEMONSTRATION

Actions speak louder than words, and the coach will find all too often that players who are at an advanced level do not always follow the basics, and can be *forced* to lose during a coaching session. I have found the following method of demonstration to be most illuminating and instructive for pupils, even at this advanced level.

Hit up, then play what I like to think of as a warm-up set with both coach and player using their respective repertoires of shots, but with the coach adjusting his level to, or a little above that of the player. It is of little consequence who wins this set.

Then play another set, and without the pupil's knowledge, the coach plays no other shot except to a length down the wall. If the ball is on the forehand, he returns down the forehand side wall, and down the left-hand wall if received on the backhand side—even accepting the penalty of conceding a point if, to make good the return, any other shot would have been required. Most generally the set will be won by the coach. But does he, in fact, win? No!

Most pupils will look with amazement if asked who won, for to them the question is irrelevant. The question seems less ridiculous when it is pointed out that, throughout the rally, you played only one type of shot (forehand and backhand being considered one), but that shot was played to a length. The coach had been content to control the ball into the corners and allow his pupil to make the errors, and lose. Ball control has been demonstrated convincingly.

Immediately play another set and inform the pupil that you intend to employ the same tactics as before, the only difference being that this time he knows exactly where the ball is going even before you hit it. With the coach controlling the ball to an immaculate length, close to the wall, and into the corners, most pupils beat themselves by "losing." They have been shown the importance of ball control, and have experienced the pressures applied, and the problems to be solved when the ball is played to a length into the back corners

BASIC BALL CONTROL

In being able to direct your service and return to a position in the back corner which leaves the pupil little opportunity to attack, you have demonstrated in the above exercise ball control in its most basic form.

This, for me, is the most dramatic demonstration of all in coaching, and is the reason why ball control and stroke production have pride of place on my list of qualities required of a good squash player. The rest of the attributes pale into insignificance if a player cannot hit the ball where he wants. (See Figure 9.) Throughout a match you should give your opponent every opportunity to make errors, being content to play a patient, waiting game, or, as will be discussed at length in a later chapter, playing *percentage squash*, where, in the final analysis, you don't have to *win*—but to make sure you do not beat yourself, and *lose*.

Ball Speed

The speed at which the ball travels is dependent upon: string tension; coordinated

FIGURE 9   Mohibullah Khan (Pakistan) against G. Hunt (Australia) with an apparent exaggerated follow-through, but the position of the eyes of both players indicates that the ball has gone high cross court. Fine balance by Khan, and anticipation by Hunt.

control of trunk, shoulders, foream, and wrist; pace of the on-coming ball; and whether it is stroked flat or with slice.

A loosely strung racket allows the ball to stay on the strings longer, as they give rather than act as a compressor to the ball, which by its very construction must *squash* to achieve maximum speed—action, followed by reaction. Let the racket work for you by having it strung tightly.

Power through Coordination

Power for the stroke is achieved through coordinated control of body movement and swing. It is helped by maintaining a balanced stance, always leaning in to the ball at the point of impact. There may be times during a match when the ball is hit off the wrong foot, especially when attacking the *early* ball (this is discussed later); but irrespective of which foot, move into every stroke to maintain control, balance, mobility and position.

Preparation for the ground stroke can be likened to winding up a spring as the racket is taken back, the spring being unwound on the forward movement, with maximum power being applied to the ball when it is struck opposite the knee. A good follow-through from the moment of impact ensures longer ball/strings contact, and continues the free-flowing movement which is so important in control and speed. (See Figure 10.)

Coaches should emphasize the importance of the *spring theory*, the necessity for a high backswing, and good follow-through. A common fault is the abrupt termination of the stroke after contact has been made with the ball, particularly on the backhand, but this can quite easily be detected and corrected by the coach. The pupil who does not follow through

FIGURE 10   The follow-through has commenced after a side-wall drive. Points to note: good balance; knees bent; eyes on the ball; racket head above the wrist; after impact the racket head is pulling the wrist around to smooth the follow-through action.

can be conditioned by demonstrating that, if he stood on a swivel, was wound-up, and then made a stroke, he would turn through 360 degrees. While it is not possible, nor in fact, desirable, for him to do this, the complete unwinding of the spring (racket travel) is approximately 180 degrees from start to finish.

Wrist

The wrist forms an important part in ball control and speed, but when considering the role played by the wrist in stroke production, we cannot consider it in isolation from the grip, for wrist and grip form a combined package. When playing, the racket is held firmly, but no more firmly than is necessary, and is only gripped tightly immediately prior to impact. If the racket were held in a vicelike grip throughout, cramp of the forearm would soon develop.

The Grip on Impact

A ball hit with a loose or *floppy* wrist lacks speed and control, but of considerably more importance is the risk of spraining the wrist. This injury occurs more often than is generally realized, but need not—no, *will* not—happen if the racket is held correctly and tightly when striking the ball.

Coaches should be aware of this, and should stress the importance to pupils. To demonstrate, have the pupil grip the racket firmly in front of his body. Ask him to then grip tightly. The tightening of the grip will have the effect of pulling the hand above the wrist and with it the racket head—the correct position. As the downward swing commences, the arc of the curve begins to flatten, and at the same time the wrist is *cocked* and locked at point of impact. Hit late, the ball could strike the floor or tin; hit early, it would go higher up the front wall than is desired, or even out of court.

Problems of the Follow-through

On the backhand in particular will the coach find pupils *pushing* from the point of impact, rather than following through. This has the effect of causing the wrist to curve outwards. The fault can be corrected by getting the pupil to:

- Grip the racket tightly immediately prior to striking the ball.

- Allow the racket head to pull the wrist around after contact.

I have achieved success in correcting the push by encouraging the pupil to think of the racket head as being on the end of a string. I ask him, instead of trying to concentrate on the swing, point of impact, follow-through, etc., to hit the ball while trying to throw the racket head away. This *throwing* action continues to the end of the follow-through.

THE SPINNING BALL

The sliced and undercut ball is not used frequently enough, or intelligently enough, to bestow the immense benefits that can accrue from this technique in stroke production.

Before discussing this aspect of the game it will be worthwhile to recapitulate, and to reflect upon the basics of stroke making—hitting the *flat* ball. To make comparison easier for the reader, this will be followed by the details involved in, and strategies demanded from, the use of the spin.

Play the Angles

The whole philosophy of the game is built upon angles—racket face to ball, ball to walls, body to walls, body to floor, etc.—so one should not build into one's game any unnecessary angle which has to be altered to accommodate another position or stroke. Stick to the basics and keep it simple. This is where the orthodox grip becomes so important. To be correct, one *shakes hands* with the racket, holding it with a cocked wrist and slightly extended forefinger.

Grip

Having learned the orthodox grip, you may find it necessary to change it slightly for the sake of comfort, but don't keep changing. It is imperative that you develop an understanding of the angle of racket face that is being presented to the ball for any shot. This is a fundamental part of ball control.

As you gain experience the grip may be varied to enable you to play *your* game. It will be seen from illustrations in this book that my grip is quite unorthodox; but it is one which suits, is comfortable, and enables me to get greater whip out of the racket, so imparting deceptive spin to the ball. Also, the shortened grip allows me to *mask* the shot more effectively.

Many great players have a grip all their own. Hashim Khan holds his racket high up on the handle as did Mohibullah Khan Snr, and that great left-hander, Jonah Barrington, keeps the forefinger inside the thumb.

Using the standard, or shake-hands grip means that you are presenting the flat face of the racket to the ball at the moment of impact for both forehand and backhand. There is no need, nor, in fact, is there time, to change the grip for a stroke on one side of the body or the other. All other angles are related to this basic racket-head angle.

Optimum Point of Impact

In the discussion on ground strokes, it was stated that the optimum point of impact is opposite the forward knee. It is at this point that the best power/control can be obtained and it is precisely the spot where the flat face of the racket is presented to the ball—the downward arc of the swing will have finished and the upward swing of the follow-through will commence. Precision such as this cannot be achieved if the grip is wrong. You should know exactly where this flat racket-face position occurs, and use this knowledge to: (a) deliberately play cross-court shots, boasts, reverse boasts, and lobs; and (b) correct any mishitting problems that affect your drives down the wall.

The effects of an incorrectly timed stroke will become apparent if you consider the swing prior to impact, and upon follow-through. Assuming that the swing is correct, the ball that is hit late for the side-wall shot will have a lower trajectory, whereas the one played early will, because of the upward movement at the commencement of the

follow-through, and opening of the racket face, be sent too high on to the front wall.

Be Deliberate and Positive

Mistiming the ball on the other strokes will have the effect of changing the angular travel. It is the angles that must be used to advantage, played deliberately, with you being in full control of the situation. Apply authority to the movement by ensuring that you hit through the ball in the direction you want it to travel rather than simply allowing it to strike the strings.

Be positive in every shot you make, be it a hard drive down the wall, boast, cross-court, high lob, or the slow delicate drop shot.

The sliced ball is such an effective weapon in a player's armory that it is surprising that so little attention is given to it by players and coaches alike. Used as a ground stroke, volley or service, it can be so effective in unsettling an opponent's stroke making and mental attitude throughout the entire match, that every player should know the principles of the spinning ball, its effect before and after hitting the wall, and the methods of imparting spin.

Do Not Overdo Spin

Like all other aspects of the game, the slice should not be overdone or used constantly. Variety is the essence of the surprise necessary to confuse, confound, baffle, and bustle the opponent. Spin can be an effective method of disturbing the opponent's judgement sufficiently to be of vital importance at the critical stage of a match.

The flight of the ball on its way to the front wall, and the path it takes on the return are simply but graphically illustrated in Figure 11. In order to impart spin, the stroke is played by cutting down through the ball with an open racket face. This slicing action causes the ball to spin and travel in an upward, curving trajectory.

Spin Determines Travel and Speed

The effect of spin not only determines travel but speed as well. In conformity with the law of aerodynamics, as the ball spins, it

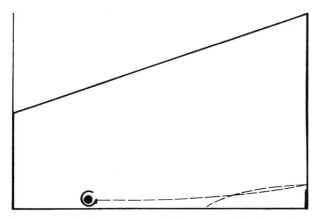

FIGURE 11   Trajectory of a spinning ball traveling to the front wall, and the path on the rebound.

builds up a boundary layer of air which moves in the same direction as the spin and tends to get dragged along with the ball, so reducing its speed. In addition, the air through which the ball travels opposes its forward movement, further restricting its speed.

Upon striking the front wall, the movement of the ball is affected by an immediate and opposite reaction caused by the spinning action. The ball rebounds on a lower plane, producing shorter *over-the-floor* travel and more rapid *fade* than the ball which is hit flat.

In Chapter 10 are demonstrated two of my favorite shots (see Figures 65b, 73b), in which I respectively aim for the nick, and fade the ball away from my opponent. I sometimes vary the action (Figure 73b) by playing closer to the right-hand corner, aiming for the nick. But, strictly speaking, the object of the slice is to accentuate the fall of the ball across the floor, and to have it bounce twice before the opponent can make a return.

Unless I specifically play for it, I do not rely upon the nick to win the rally, as this *killing* ground stroke relies for its effectiveness upon spin rather than stun or squeeze.

The Use of Spin for Placement

Except when playing the drop shot, the speed of the ball should be sharp rather than fast, for you must concentrate on playing the return away from the opponent, using spin to help in its implementation. Placement should be short of, or away from, the opponent.

Nothing is achieved (except on an easy *get* for your opponent) by hitting the ball high on to the front wall. Depending upon the state of the game, and score, I generally aim for a spot two to three inches above the tin. This obviously varies according to my opponent's position but the ball should not hit any higher than eight inches from the tin.

If the opponent has been caught back from the short line, you will need to go as low to the tin as possible to obtain the second bounce quickly and catch him flat-footed. On the other hand, if both of you are in the forecourt, it is advisable to hit higher and play deeper so that the rebound will fall beyond his reach.

It is not essential to play for the nick, but if the ball is played towards the side wall, the spinning action makes the chance of getting the nick a distinct *possibility* and not, as one hears said so often, as a *lucky* shot. Luck does not enter into it, as the type of shot played gives a better than 50 percent chance of the ball striking the nick or half-nick.

Denying the Opponent Distance and Time

It is essential that you be forever conscious of the importance of denying your opponent distance and time. The spun ball reduces the flight off the front wall, and this is where your judgment of how high to hit above the tin is critical. A low side-wall shot may get a nick, but the higher ball results in longer flight and higher bounce, and presents a fast, alert opponent with the opening to attack. However, a well-sliced ball, played with a good *masking* action from the body, and with nice placement help to deceive the opponent. It also feels good.

The first lesson I learned from Hashim Khan, which was stressed later by Amin, was: "Don't go for the killing shot all of the time." The advice was imprinted on my mind, and from then on, I have exercised patience. Nevertheless, except for the tactical reason of tiring the opponent, I always go for the kill if the opportunity presents itself. Not to do so may involve me in a long drawn-out rally which would draw upon my reserves of energy which may be needed later in the match. Even though one's level of fitness may be high, it is not wise to squander energy unnecessarily.

Playing to the Nick

The killing shot forms part of my repertoire and I am constantly looking for chances to play it irrespective of my position, sometimes throwing caution to the wind and taking a gamble in the hope that the surprise will catch my opponent on the wrong foot or out of position, or maybe shake his confidence with a side-wall nick.

I seem forever to return to Hashim, but apart from all his other qualities, he was the master of playing the kill into a side-wall nick from both forehand and backhand side. The first time we played he hit a backhand cross-court return, playing the ball with heavy slice and great power, and got the nick. I said seriously, "Lucky shot!" He went on to demonstrate that he could hit a nick at any time, from any position on the court, and from both sides. This demonstration, and the philosophy behind it, has stayed with me over the years, for it is true that while there will never be another Hashim, if you play for the nick you stand a good chance of success. But the shot must be played with heavy slice, and only when the time is right. Practice will perfect the technique, and experience determine the decision when to play the kill or not. Through practice and experimentation you can develop killing shots of your own. Let me suggest a couple of others which you can try. I have selected one backhand and one forehand.

Backhand The time comes during a side-wall rally when my opponent's ball falls short of a length and a foot or so from the side wall. Irrespective of whether he has moved back to the T or not, I then introduce the kill. I maintain the same speed of racket swing but play the ball with heavy slice down the wall, and at an angle, aiming for a spot two to three inches above the tin. The slice kills the ball on the rebound and the angle helps it slide into the side wall.

Forehand My opponent has forced me into the front forehand corner. During the match I had been inclined to reply with a drop shot but this time I hear him coming. He is alert, fast, and likely to get to a lob or drive, be it down the wall or cross-court, so I play the kill along the side wall. The ball is played about eight inches above the tin, for this time I want it to die as a medium length shot rather than land too short. The same shot played flat would have given him a better chance of making a *get*, but the slice has clouded his judgment by finishing shorter than he expected.

PERCENTAGE SQUASH

Percentage squash is the name of the game. The player who has a lower percentage of lost rallies wins the match. The end result really is not to win, rather to allow your opponent to lose. So, control the ball, placing it where you want at the speed you choose, instead of having it shoot at random all over the court. This may provide the weaker player with good exercise but is not designed to win matches.

The coach should stress the fundamentals of ball control to pupils at every level. Once the beginner has learned to hit the ball with some regularity, he must be made to concentrate upon service and the return of every ball down the side wall (backhand and forehand). As his standard improves, the other strokes can be taught, but the point must be continually made that the ball down the wall forms the base from which his future game will develop and improve.

One often finds that players, even up to a reasonably good standard, are of the opinion that the harder they hit the ball the better, giving scant thought to control and *touch*. The coach should discourage this among beginners, and demonstrate to the more advanced player the advantages of control. All should be told that unless the ball can be controlled, it cannot be hit hard with any match-winning effect. The very good players adopt this plan of play, for they realize that just one loose shot opens up an opportunity for their opponent to go into the attack. They know that other good players have the full range of shots at their disposal, and that they therefore must be content to play a waiting game, be patient, and go for the winner only when the opponent hits a loose ball.

SUMMARY

- The time to play the kill must be right.

- Recognize that the opportunity has arisen and adjust stance and position accordingly.

- Be confident that you have the ability to play the shot correctly.

- Cut down and through the ball to impart the spin.

- Decide what placement you want and aim for the right spot on the front wall.

- Play the ball as a straight line.

- Correctly hit, the sliced return denies the opponent distance and time.

- Try to mask the shot with the body.

- The chances of the ball finishing in the nick are greatly increased when spin is employed.

- If the opponent gets to the ball played with spin, he will generally play it too early due to the lower and slower trajectory.

ONE FINAL COMMENT

I continually emphasize: *"Watch the ball!"* To that one should add: *"Watch your opponent!"*

Throughout the rally the thinking player is continually presenting his opponent with problems to be solved and opportunities to make errors. The spinning ball compounds these errors and can be the vital component at a critical stage in the match, and more so if your opponent is getting a little physically and mentally tired. The speed of the game being as it is, watching ball and opponent become one in the split-second before he makes the stroke, and any slight change of movement can give you advanced warning of his intended shot. You are then better able to determine direction and speed of the ball, be it a flat or sliced return.

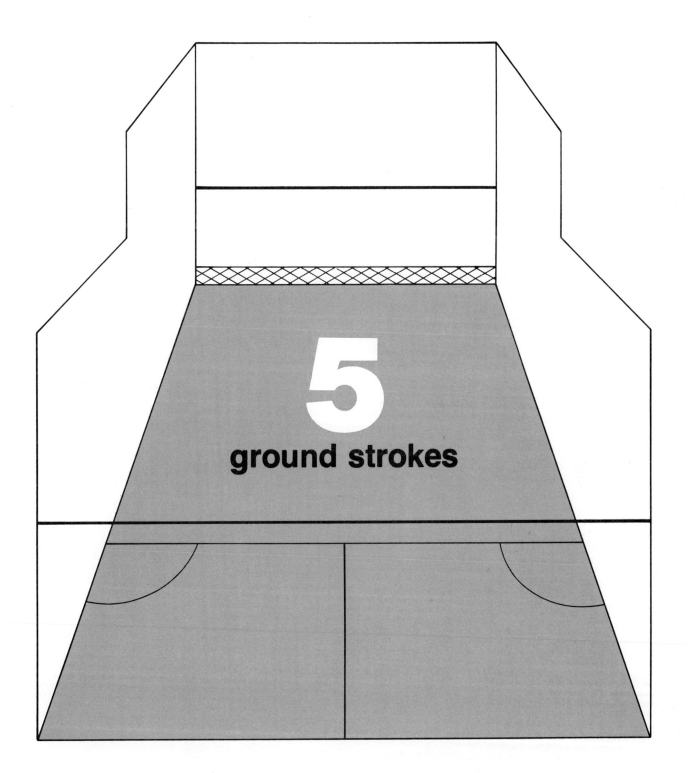

5
ground strokes

INTRODUCTION

Having discussed and demonstrated the importance of ball control, the coach logically moves on to explain and demonstrate the strokes used in the game which allow the player to place the ball where he wishes, at a speed sufficient to gain an advantage. The ground stroke is the bread-and-butter of the game.

BASIC SHOTS

Not taking into account the serve, there are five basic shots in squash:

- down the side wall
- cross-court
- boast
- drop shot
- lob.

It is from these that the whole range of variations develops.

The most basic of all is down the side wall, for with this shot played to a length, the opponent will lose more often than the player making the shot will win. The coach can demonstrate this successfully against most players, with them being both aware and unaware of the tactics being used throughout the rally.

While differences in stroke production and stance are necessary to achieve the required result, that is, at the moment of impact, a degree of commonality among the factors at work in the production of the five strokes:

- racket head above wrist
- wrist *cocked* and *locked*
- lead with the forward leg
- weight on the forward foot
- ball struck opposite front knee
- eye on the ball.

It is the player who ultimately decides how hard he wants to hit the ball, but coaches must discourage pupils from hitting hard all the time, or for that matter, only playing the soft return. Even a slight change of pace can have an unsettling effect on an opponent's timing and balance.

First I will discuss the execution of the basic shots played on the forehand. Specific differences or other items of importance will then be discussed in relation to the backhand.

FOREHAND

Backswing

Using the analogy of *winding the spring*, picture the backswing on ground strokes providing the tension necessary to generate racket speed. The speed at which he strikes the ball is determined by the player (accepting that beginners may be having difficulty with timing and control), but a smooth, high backswing with racket head high above the shoulder will help to provide rhythm to the stroke.

The backswing is commenced as the weight is transferred to the left foot, the racket being at the top of the arc before the step across is completed. (See Figure 12.) This high

FIGURE 12   At the top of the forehand backswing.

action permits greater freedom of movement, control, and power as the stroke is made. A backswing that ends below shoulder height or at waist level restricts power/control, forcing the ball into a more vertical than horizontal plane. Also, under these conditions, controlled slicing is difficult, for to impart spin the racket must be brought down with the strings cutting across the face of the ball.

Body Movement

A smooth-flowing rhythmic stroke is the result of coordinated body movement with the "spring" unwinding at a regular, even pace. The power applied to the stroke is provided by the transfer of body weight, through rotation of shoulder, trunk, hips, and arm (of which the racket is an extension). Weight is initially on the left foot, but transfers to the right after impact and follow-through, balance being achieved through the positioning of the right foot and left arm. (See Figure 13.)

From the start of the downswing to the end of follow-through, no break must occur in the continuity of the movement. Players must guard against accentuating the swing on

FIGURE 13   Just after the point of impact for the side-wall shot.

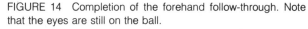

FIGURE 14   Completion of the forehand follow-through. Note that the eyes are still on the ball.

follow-through because of the danger of hitting their opponent. It is equally important for coaches to advise pupils against finishing the swing just prior to impact, pushing at, rather than stroking the ball. The end result would be a decrease in both power and control. (See Figure 14.)

Side-Wall Shot

Irrespective of whether the player is returning service, or retrieving during the rally, the correct sequence of stroke-production movements remains the same, following a smooth well-defined rhythmic pattern. Variations will, and must, occur to enable the player to cope as changing circumstances are encountered, and these will be explained. However, the coach must always ensure correctness in stroking, and aim for perfection. At our first meeting, I tell a pupil that I intend to teach him the proper way to stroke the ball, indicating that only when he knows how to play correctly can he make a reflex shot if caught on the wrong foot or off-balance.

The sequence is:

1. Eye on the ball—always.

2. From a position of even balance on both feet (with the weight on the toes), transfer the weight to the left foot as the step across to the right is made.

3. This movement of the feet, with the accompanying rotation of the whole body and the circular backswing of arm and racket places the player in a position facing the side wall. The spring is now fully wound, with the racket in position to flatten the arc of the swing on the unwind, in the direction of the intended stroke.

4. The knees are bent at a comfortable angle to allow for further movement and mobility. The left leg leads, the foot facing the side wall (and a little to the front), but the player's stance should be neither too narrow nor wide. Either extreme affects weight shift and balance. In order to achieve the ideal of striking the ball opposite the left knee, the extent of knee bend will be determined by the height of ball bounce. It should be appreciated that if the racket head is to be kept above the wrist at the moment of impact, this can only be achieved by bending. Knees and racket head can be considered to move in unison in relation to the height of the ball from the floor.

5. Trunk and shoulders lean into the stroke. In this position, before the unwind, the coach stops the action of his pupil to point out its correctness or otherwise, to make necessary changes and explain the "Whys."

6. The force applied to the ball will be a combination of factors, resulting from the correct execution of body, shoulder and arm movement during the unwind. Maximum forward velocity of the racket head occurs when it is facing the intended direction of flight of the ball. From the high position at the top of the backswing, the racket flattens during the arc of its travel, until the face is nearly at a right-angle to the floor at the point of impact.

7. The grip is firm throughout, tightening just before the ball is struck.

8. From the start of the swing until the point of impact, the wrist is pulling the racket through. (See Figure 15.) Then as the follow-through commences, the racket head pulls the wrist around, smoothing out the action. (See Figure 16.) Coaches must instill in pupils the need to keep away from, and not crowd, the ball, thus ensuring that contact is made with the arm in an extended position.

9. Follow-through should bring the racket head up and not around in a wide extended arc. The latter, apart from being dangerous, would impair balance and the regaining of position. Upon completion of the follow-through, the weight should be evenly distributed on both feet, with the player facing the front wall ready to move to, and reply to, his opponent's return.

37

FIGURE 15 Hitting the low forehand shot down the wall. Knees are bent; balance is good; eyes are on the ball; the wrist is cocked and is pulling the racket head around.

FIGURE 16 Follow-through has commenced from a nice low, crouched, body position. The wrist has unlocked allowing the racket head to pull it around and so smooth the action, but note that the wrist is still cocked and the eyes are still on the ball.

Cross-court

The cross-court shot is played in a manner similar to that down the side wall, varying only in stance. Instead of standing facing squarely to the side wall, the player positions himself at an angle, the direction of ball travel being dependent upon this angular movement of the body.

As the ball has to travel further from the player to reach the front wall than when the side-wall shot is played, a ball which would strike just above the tin when played down the side needs to be hit higher to make good the return when struck at the same speed. This is the most frequent fault encountered, and leaves players wondering why the top of the tin is so often hit. It is easily corrected when the reason for error is understood, and the shot supports an excellent case for slicing the sharply angled low return—the upward trajectory of the spinning ball and the resultant reaction off the front wall increase the possibility of finding the side-wall nick.

Boast

Anybody who has ever watched the champions play cannot have failed to notice that for every one-hundred shots played, ninety-nine went straight up and down the wall. Good players cannot afford to make a mistake for they know that their opponents have a full repertoire of shots and are waiting for the chance to try a winner.

A good shot down, and close to, the wall presents an opponent with: (a) very little ball to hit at; (b) a lot of wall to contend with; (c) the back-corner problem. Against this consider the comparative ease of coping with a boasted return.

The Luxury of Time The shortest distance between two points is a straight line. Distance is time—and time to get to and play the ball is the luxury you must deny your opponent.

The boasted ball finishes its travel near the front wall and presents an alert receiver with the opportunity to either play a winner or go into attack. The ability to boast effectively forms a no less important part of a player's range of strokes than any other. The knowledge of *how* to play the shot from any position on the court must be acquired, and it is the action of stroking the ball which is all-important. Rather than flattening the arc or cutting through the ball during the swing, the boast is achieved by hitting the ball against the side wall using an upward movement of the racket. This action sends it on a rising trajectory from the side to the front wall, but as a result of sheer force, the harder the ball is hit, the less defined will be the upward motion.

Playing the Angles   Angles are an important aspect of the boast and only from practice will the player know where to hit the ball on to the side wall for it to reach a certain spot up front. As a general guide for the boast taken at the back of the court, the nearer to the back wall the ball strikes the side wall, the closer it will be to a nick on the opposite front wall. Conversely, a ball that strikes the wall further to the front will land mid-court.

When coaching beginners in boasting practice, I have them stand half-way back from the short line, facing the side wall. Hitting to their forehand I have them boast the return by hitting the side wall at the point about three feet up from where the *short* line meets the wall. There is no need for them to hit hard at this stage, for a boast made with the correct action will have an inevitable result—the ball must reach the front wall. With practice the pupil will soon develop the action, gaining confidence as he goes.

Hitting the Late Ball   What the pupil is doing in the above exercise, in effect, is hitting the ball late in order to send it on its angular course. This fact should be made known to him by the coach. This *lateness* is an important factor to remember, for there are times during a rally when the player running for the ball finds it has passed the optimum point of impact. A side-wall or cross-court shot cannot be made, and the only shot left is the boast. (See Figure 17.)

The Back-corner Problem   The lob service or return that falls into the back corner fills the inexperienced (and sometimes semiprofi-

FIGURE 17   The ball has gone past the player, and he is left with only one shot—the boast of the late ball. To try to hit down the wall or cross court would be futile.

cient) player with a mild form of panic, but correctly handled it should not instill quite so many fears in them. With the ball in this position the player must boast to make good the return. He is very much on the defensive, the opponent holding every advantage, but may I once again stress that, once the return goes *up*, your opponent has the problem of return—you have solved his problems for the rally if you fail to get the ball back.

The boast from the back corner (see Figures 18, 19, and 20) requires the same action as that from any other position on the court, but to achieve success:

FIGURE 18   Forehand boast from the back corner showing backswing, with the left leg facing the corner.

39

FIGURE 19 Forehand back-corner boast at the point of impact. The ball has been hit with an upward swing so as to produce the right trajectory to enable it to reach the front wall.

FIGURE 20 Completion of the follow-through from the back-corner boast. The body has swung around to follow the path of the ball and to ensure quick movement up to the front.

- play the shot facing the corner;
- also point the left leg and foot to the corner;
- do not crowd the ball; and
- keep the ball at arm's length.

So, adopting these four principles, the movement is into the ball, stroking with the same upward action as before, allowing the body to swing further around on the follow-through, to face the front wall upon completion of the stroke. The correct action will position the body naturally.

The most common fault found among players executing the back-corner boast, even when the action and stance have been mastered, is crowding the ball. A cramped stroke reduces control and accuracy, and a ball struck under these circumstances will rarely go up. It is far better to fall into the stroke rather than back away. Unless forced into a defensive position when no other shot is possible, use the boast sparingly. It can be an excellent form of surprise and attack, but only if not overdone. And if you have to boast out of the back corner, get back to the T as quickly as possible to be in position for your opponent's return.

Reverse Boast As the normal boast is played onto the side wall facing the player, the reverse boast uses the opposite side wall, the ball being hit flat rather than with an upward swing. As the disadvantages far outweigh any advantage to be gained, the use of this shot should be severely restricted. Played from a back-court position, the ball has a long way to travel before reaching the front wall, moving then to the center of the court. When played from near the front of the court, you have an acute angle to work with and will find the percentage of errors to be high.

Back-wall Boast The best advice I can give about playing this shot is—do not. No player should ever get himself into a position where this shot has to be attempted. Note that I used the word *attempted*, for that is all it is—an attempt. The time it takes the ball to reach the front wall is so long that the opponent is given the opening for a winner.

Drop Shot

Before discussing the drop shot, one point should be cleared up. It is a shot that is stroked as is any other ground stroke (but with important differences which will be explained), and is not pushed or poked as many inexperienced players attempt to do on both the forehand and backhand sides.

It is true that, to reach the top level, a player must possess all nine qualities listed in the first chapter. It is equally important to remember that a good drop shot cannot be executed unless one possesses the first four qualities—the ball must be controlled; great concentration is demanded; to get down for the shot requires flexibility from the body (mobility); and mobility is a by-product of fitness and training.

Touch and Mobility My whole game is styled upon that of the Pakistanis, relying not only upon power but also on touch, with a need for body flexibility when playing strokes, rather than playing from the upright and rigid position which most Europeans seem to favor in their approach to stroke production. The drop shot is undoubtedly the most delicate shot in the game and is a vital part of the repertoire for any player hoping to reach the top.

It is an attacking weapon—never defensive. As an element of surprise, the drop shot can be played from the back half of the court, either straight or cross-court, but played only rarely—and certainly never before the third game, as the opponent will still be comparatively fresh. To be effective the ball must travel slowly, and if played from the back gives your opponent plenty of time to get into position and reply with a killing shot.

Front-half Court Shot The shot must be considered then, as one played only from the front half of the court and when the opponent is deep in the back half, often as a reply to a boast. Clearly, to play an attacking shot such as a drop demands balance and the athletic ability to get down to the ball. However, if the correct fitness-training program is undertaken, this physical capacity is not beyond any player. (Fitness training is dealt with in detail in Chapter 11.)

Line of Flight For the drop shot you must get right down to the ball and so ensure precise control over the stroke. (See Figure 21.) Greater accuracy is achieved if you keep the ball and the aiming point more or less in the same line from the eye. It becomes apparent that the more direct your aim, the more

FIGURE 21 The drop shot played from a crouched position, knees bent, forward leg toward the corner. Note the good line from the eyes, through the ball, to the aiming point.

accurate will be the shot. So the line of flight for the ball must be from the eye, through the ball to the aiming point.

To get down as illustrated, and remain balanced, requires that a great deal of strength be developed in the thigh muscles, but this positioning is essential to success. I generally play the forehand drop shot to the forehand corner, but once again, to add variety to my game and continually keep my opponent guessing, I occasionally play cross-court. (See Figures 22 and 23.)

Memory Bank The key points to remember when playing the forehand drop shot are.

1. Get down to the ball and take up a good well-balanced stance.

2. The weight should be on the left foot with the knee pointing in the direction of the intended shot. (See Figure 24.) In this position complete balance is maintained with the right

FIGURE 22 Opponent has played an excellent cross-court drop shot and caught me going the wrong way. Note the open racket face necessary to impart spin to the ball.

FIGURE 23 I position the body to play a backhand cross-court drop shot. At the last minute, and by delaying the shot, I play to the left-hand corner and catch opponent going the wrong way.

FIGURE 24 The drop shot has been played with the knees bent. The ball has been masked from the opponent by the player's body.

leg and left arm enabling you to return quickly to the T upon completion of the shot.

3. The ball is struck just in front of the left knee.

4. Take a short or half backswing, but make sure you stroke the ball and do not push or poke. The follow-through, like the backswing, is shortened, but nevertheless forms an important part of the stroke making.

5. Open the racket face before it reaches the point of impact to impart spin to the ball. The spin sends the ball on an upward trajectory, takes the pace off it, and makes it die sooner.

6. Keep the wrist cocked and locked throughout, and be sure to keep the racket head above the wrist.

7. Play the ball to hit the front wall first, aiming for a point two to three inches above

the tin and one foot from the side wall. Playing to this spot will achieve a rebound close to the nick at the side wall, but even at the worst, you can expect the ball to fade along the wall and die. The ball played to the side wall first rebounds into center court, giving the opponent more chance of making a return—and maybe a winner.

8. The drop shot played to the same side as the stroke, i.e. forehand to the right corner, is the easiest and most effective. It has less distance to travel, takes less time than the cross-court, but is of equal importance, if the shot is played badly; for example, if it is played too high and too far out, the chances are that the ball will still end its travel somewhere near the side wall, making it difficult for the opponent. On the other hand, the cross-court drop shot played badly is more likely to end up in the middle of the court, and once again present the opponent with the chance to play a "kill" return.

Backhand Drop Shot A short commentary on the backhand drop shot may be pertinent at this stage before the backhand is discussed in greater detail.

Because of the need to get down to play the drop shot, and the physical construction of the body, the backhand stroke is easier to play than the forehand. The method of playing the shot is the same, but the ball is played in front of the right knee (for the forehand it was the left knee), and there is a freer flow of backswing, stroking, and follow-through, which means that greater accuracy can be achieved on this side. (See Figure 25.)

Volley Drop Shot An effective combination shot is the volley drop, in which the volley is generally taken around the short line (taken as the *early* ball) being played into either front corner. Playing this shot creates an element of surprise for the opponent, who, if he happens to be in the back of the court, will find it almost impossible to retrieve. (See Figure 26.)

Common Faults Some of the most common faults found when playing the drop shot are:

● The player stands too square-on to either the front wall or side wall instead of angling the leading leg and body so that the shot can be played toward the corner.

● Failure to bend down and align the eyes and ball onto the chosen aiming point. By remaining too upright and rigid the player decreases the accuracy and quite often hits the tin. (See Figure 27.)

FIGURE 25 Superb backhand drop-shot action by opponent. Compare this with Figure 21 and note the similarity, which is the result of good coaching and practice.

FIGURE 26 I fail to get down to the forehand drop shot, so accuracy is jeopardized. The ball has been hit too high above the tin; too close to the side wall. An easy *get* for opponent.

FIGURE 27 The ball has been played with a flat racket head, has too much pace, and lacks accuracy. Once again an easy get.

• Pushing at or poking the ball rather than stroking it with a short backswing, and correspondingly short follow-through.

• Playing the ball with a flat racket head. The racket must be open at point of impact to impart spin and so take the pace off the ball, making it fade and die into the nick. (See Figure 28.)

FIGURE 28   Forehand volley drop shot played to the right-hand corner with the opponent flat-footed in the back of the court.

So remember, the drop shot is an attacking weapon, played with touch, and most usually from the front half of the court. It is *not* a defensive shot.

Lob

Most top coaches and players agree that the lob is probably the most underrated and underestimated stroke in the game. So few players give thought to this shot, but used correctly it can constitute both attack and defense for the young, fit, top-level player, as well as for the more mature exponent. (See Chapter 12.)

When to Play It   When I get into trouble at the front of the court, or when I have rushed for the short ball or boast, or at any time when I get into difficulties near the front wall, I play the lob. This forces my opponent deep into the back corner and allows me some little time to recover to the T. A good high lob into the lights and against a dark-colored roof will cause the ball to be lost for a split-second and so impair the opponent's judgment. Very few players can handle the high backhand return with any confidence, being merely content to play a safe return. So be aware that this is the hardest shot of all, and lob to this side for maximum advantage. (See Figure 29.)

Whether lobbing in desperation, changing the pace of the game, or forcing my opponent into the back of the court, I hit the ball softly but remember at the same time that *height is the most important feature.* (See Figures

FIGURE 29   Forehand cross-court lob that will rebound off the front wall and side wall and behind the service box on the backhand side. I have got down to the ball and played it with an upward sweep to achieve height.

30 and 31.) If the lob is played down the side, try to keep the ball as close to the wall as possible and aim to have it land in the corner. Such a ball presents the opponent with many problems—the ball is high until at the end of its travel; he has a lot of wall to contend with; having taken the pace off the ball, you have compounded his back-corner problem. (See Figures 32 and 33.)

FIGURE 31   Backhand cross-court lob played too low.

FIGURE 30   Forehand cross-court lob is too low and will present the opponent with an easy winner.

Attack and Defense   The cross-court lob is also used for both attack and defense, but in playing this shot I aim to have the ball rebound from the front onto the side wall, high up and beyond the rear of the service box. Any pace will have been taken off the ball, confining it even more to the back of the court. (See Figures 34 and 35.)

The stroke is made with an open racket face, hitting through the ball with an upward action. Weight must be on the leading foot, and a good follow-through is essential even if

you are playing off balance. And even when playing on the wrong foot or off balance, make sure that the upward action and follow-through are good, so as to achieve height and thus prevent the opponent from cutting off the ball.

Play Safe   When stretching for the ball up front it is inadvisable to try any fancy shot, attempted winner, or drop shot. The chance of success is minimal and you can only compound the percentage of error. Play safe and lob, straight or cross-court; regain the T (and your composure), being content to defend for the present, and go into the attack later. But that good defensive lob finishes many times as a fine attacking shot, and even if your direction is astray and the path of the ball is back over the T, the opponent who has followed you to the front will have some difficulty in attacking.

Advantages of the Attacking Lob   The attacking lob, while played mostly from the front of the court, can be played from any-

FIGURE 32   Forehand lob down the wall played from near the front of the court. Opponent is moving back to make a return but the player can regain command of the T.

FIGURE 33   Backhand lob down the wall. Good height from the ball achieved by the upswept action and follow-through.

46

FIGURE 34 Backhand cross-court lob. The stance is more square on to the front wall than when playing down the side wall.

FIGURE 35 Attempted backhand cross-court lob, but I am facing the corner. However, if the ball is hit with height, and travels over the center of the court, the opponent will encounter difficulties.

where, and has several advantages: far greater control and accuracy can be achieved when playing the ball softly rather than hitting it hard; it introduces a good change of pace which can break up the opponent's game and concentration; it enables you to recover some breath during a long rally; it forces the opponent to play a shot instead of reacting more easily to the hard-hit ball; it makes the opponent do a little more work, which can be the vital element near the end of a long match; and on a cold court where the ball dies more readily, a good lob can turn out to be an outright winner.

So do not underrate or underestimate the lob as a shot—to be used as attack or defense—that forces the opponent into the back of the court.

BACKHAND

The simple statement, "The backhand is merely a forehand in reverse" may be correct in basic terms (and I do advise coaches to instruct pupils along these lines to allay any apprehension they may have about playing a backhand shot), but because one is hitting the ball on the left side of the body there are physical differences. Nevertheless differences do not necessarily mean difficulties, and a better backhand than forehand can be turned to advantage in a match, as most opponents will play to this side hoping to force an error. (See Figure 36.)

The Psychological Barrier

Personally I favor the backhand. It allows complete freedom of movement from the top of the backswing to follow-through when, upon completion of the stroke, the racket head is traveling in an arc away from the body. (See Figure 37.) Against this, the trunk presents a shield on the forehand follow-through, with the shoulder muscles tending to bunch up, creating a resistance. I believe therefore that the backhand is more a psychological barrier than anything else, and should be recognized and taught as such by coaches.

FIGURE 36 Jonah Barrington (G.B.), the world's leading left-hander, displaying beautiful balance and stance in playing a backhand. Barrington's stance and Torsam Khan's (Pakistan) movement indicate that the ball is going cross court.

Any stroke can present problems, be it from the right or left, unless correctly played—and the backhand is no exception. As the correct positioning and stance for the forehand have already been described, only the differences for the backhand need be shown and emphasized.

Boast

But notwithstanding the above, I believe there could be merit in going into more detail for the backhand boast played both as a ground stroke and volley. I like to think of the boast as being mostly defensive, but it can be a fine attacking shot that is given too little attention by coaches and players alike. When the opponent has you on the run to the side or back of the court, the defensive boast may be played, but this could be the time to go into attack and possibly spring a surprise. (See Figure 38.)

Aiming Point The object is to get the boasted ball to end its flight as near to the opposite front corner, and a nick, as possible. With practice this can be achieved. The ball

must follow a path that results in it hitting the front wall two to three inches above the tin, and avoids at all costs the possibility of it rebounding back into the center of the court from where the opponent is able to not only reach it but to attempt a winner.

Very little percentage is to be gained if your opponent is in the front half of the court when the boast is made. Best results can be achieved when you have forced him deep, and then move quickly to cut off his return. The volley boast is an effective weapon as it interrupts the flow of the rally, possibly disrupting his anticipation, and maybe catching him on the wrong foot.

FIGURE 37   High cross-court backhand shot. The racket face is slightly open and the eyes are following the ball.

FIGURE 38   I move late to the ball and have to boast. There is no other shot available, but the balance is excellent, and the good racket/arm position ensures maximum power and control. Eyes are on the ball as I lean into the shot. Opponent's anticipation is good as he moves to the forehand front corner.

Correct Stroking　Angles are all-important in playing the boast but remember, for the ball to get up and not hit the tin it must be struck with an open racket face and upward action to produce the correct trajectory. This upward action decreases in importance as power is increased.

The stroke starts at the shoulder with power coming from the elbow, which puts sharpness into the stroke. Be careful to keep the wrist cocked and locked until the follow-through commences. (See Figures 39, 40, and 41.) The center of gravity of my body is well

FIGURE 40　Backhand boast is just after point of impact.

FIGURE 41　Backhand boast follow-through. High action has sent the ball on an upward trajectory. The player's body has come around with the shot and so enables him to quickly regain his position up front.

FIGURE 39　Backswing for the backhand boast out of the corner. Racket is high above the left shoulder; knees bent; body leaning into the shot; stance away from the ball for freedom of swing.

forward with weight on the right leg whenever I play an offensive boast, or when I have been forced to boast the late ball. (See Figure 38.)

Perseverance and Practice　Unless you, like me, have a better backhand than forehand, you will find the backhand boast to be a difficult shot to master, but perseverance, concentration, and practice will produce results.

Do not attempt to graduate to the volley boast until you have mastered the boast as a ground stroke and can play it with assurance. (Figure 42.)

Weight transference, body movement, and backswing are the same as for the forehand (but in reverse; for example, right foot across), with the racket head taken high above the left shoulder—the complete winding of the spring. When instructing beginners, I get them to stop at the end of the backswing so that I can correct the stance:

51

FIGURE 42 Backhand volley boast. Opponent has anticipated a shot down the wall and has been *wrong-footed* by this shot.

- knees bent;

- right leg leading; body at 90 degrees to the intended direction of the shot;

- body bent forward with the right shoulder leaning towards the right knee;

- right elbow at an angle of approximately 30 degrees to the floor. At this angle, the racket head flattens into a natural arc on the downswing, being nearly at 90 degrees to the floor at point of impact. There is a tendency among beginners to have the elbow parallel to the floor.

- In this static position, I have my pupils note that if the racket were taken back just a little further, the left shoulder would be hit by the shaft some four inches down from the throat.

- The *unwind* is the same as a forehand. From the top of the backswing to the point of impact the wrist pulls the racket head through; as follow-through commences the player allows the racket to pull the wrist around, so smoothing the swing.

Problems

Problems encountered in playing the backhand are similar to those discussed earlier, but in the course of experience, I have come across some peculiarities in shots from this side of the body:

Problem The player misses the ball or mishits into the ceiling.

Solution Either one of, or a combination of two factors—racket backswing to below

52

shoulder level, and/or the elbow too high. Starting the swing from below shoulder level results in the racket striking the ball with an open face, whereas a higher (and correct) backswing allows the player to flatten the arc on the unwind. The beginner has neither control nor experience to effectively play the backhand from the high-elbow position, even if he wished to. The speed with which the racket arm moves does not allow time to move from the near-horizontal to a near-vertical plane. Result—the player misses the ball.

Problem The swing is correct to the point of impact—then the player *pushes* at the ball.

Solution Both control of the ball and power for the stroke are severely restricted when using the *push*, and there is the added danger of spraining the wrist. As coach I have found this to be one of the errors that have given me most problems in devising a solution, as the push, once developed, is quite persistent. Success has been achieved by getting the player to concentrate on seemingly *throwing* the racket head in an arc from the start of the downswing to the end of the follow-through. It is immaterial at the start of the problem-solving session whether or not he hits the ball, or whether it goes where he wishes, so long as the action is smoothed out. Control and power will follow.

The coach will notice that the wrist curves outward in the push rather than being concave as when *cocked* and *locked*. Throwing the racket head changes the convex wrist.

GROUND-STROKE PROBLEMS AND SOLUTIONS

The coach will encounter faults in stroke making and be called upon to detect and eradicate errors even up to (and sometimes including) advanced players. More patience is required with the beginner, who may lack ball sense and coordination, but the test of a coach's expertise is in helping the experienced player who

realizes that smoothing out some seemingly minor point will mean the difference between improving and winning, or remaining at the same standard.

The following collection of problems and solutions is by no means complete, but it represents a selection of the most common faults I have encountered, and the methods I use to correct these faults. Especially in the case of the beginner, the ball that does not go as he intends may be a combination of errors. However, I will try to highlight only one fault in each stroke, leaving the coach to use his own knowledge in solving the complete problem.

Problem By far the most common fault among beginners is that of trying to play a ground stroke without moving the left foot across for a forehand, and the right foot for a backhand.

Solution Demonstrate at the start of every coaching session how the foot should be placed, coordinating this with the backswing. The pupil will feel the restriction in the shoulder in taking a full backswing without moving the feet in comparison with the freedom when the stance is correct.

The use of key words, repeated over and over again during stroke-making practice helps remind the pupil until he reaches the stage where correct action becomes instinctive. I recommend such "keys" as: *Foot across*, as preparation for the stroke is made; *High backswing; Knees bent; Tight grip; Rotate.* These key words are certainly not all used during one stroke as this would be as impractical as it would be confusing. Concentrate on one aspect at a time; for example, at the time when the foot should be moved into position say, "Across" just before the step should be made. Cover one aspect during a number of practice strokes before emphasizing the next key word, and ensure that the word is said immediately prior to the action.

Problem The ball travels into the opposite front wall.

Solution The most general cause among beginners is striking the ball too early, with the result that it follows the natural line of the racket face. This is brought about by an incorrect stance and/or hurrying the shot. By correcting the stance and instructing the pupil to delay hitting the ball, the coach can easily solve this problem.

For the more advanced player, whose stance is basically correct, the problem is generally a matter of timing, which can generally be coupled to fitness, and of not picking the *sliced* return. As standards improve, so does the pace of the game. Although watching his opponent strike the ball, a player may not have detected the slice. The brain computes ball speed assuming a flat stroke and on the basis of the previous shots in the rally. But the mechanics of flight for the spinning ball result in its movement through the air being slower, causing impact to be made too early.

Problem The balls sprayed in indiscriminate directions.

Solution This can be any one of, or a combination of factors, but mostly I have found lack of control attributable in the main to: (a) failure to cock and lock the wrist at the point of impact, and/or (b) allowing the racket head to fall below the level of the wrist.

In (b) the player may take a firm and vice-like grip but forget another vital factor—bending the knees and getting down to the ball. The coach therefore looks for: locked and cocked wrist; racket head above the wrist; bent knees.

Problem Off balance during and after stroke making.

Solution Obviously an incorrect stance is the overriding factor.

By adopting the correct and balanced stance, with the weight on the leading foot, and stability maintained by the other foot and left arm, the coach can demonstrate quite effectively how far the body can move forward, or back, and still leave the player room to make a well-controlled shot. For a person of average height the amount of movement is something in the order of two feet forward or back before the balance is lost. (See Figure 43.) On the other hand, the same person topples over very quickly when both feet are evenly spaced, but parallel, and the legs are kept stiff.

FIGURE 43 Perfect balance. By taking up the correct stance, I have given myself great flexibility in stroke-making plus a wider choice of shots. This time I choose a hard low cross-court shot, aiming for the nick.

Problem Returns hit high, uncontrolled on the front wall and/or ceiling, or continually hit the tin.

Solution Invariably the grip is wrong. Players using an incorrect grip look strained and awkward when stroking the ball. The coach will have no problems in detecting where this fault lies, because of the awkward attitude.

The above are just some of the problems common to all ground strokes. Of course not every problem could be covered in this or any other book, but this selection should help both player and coach.

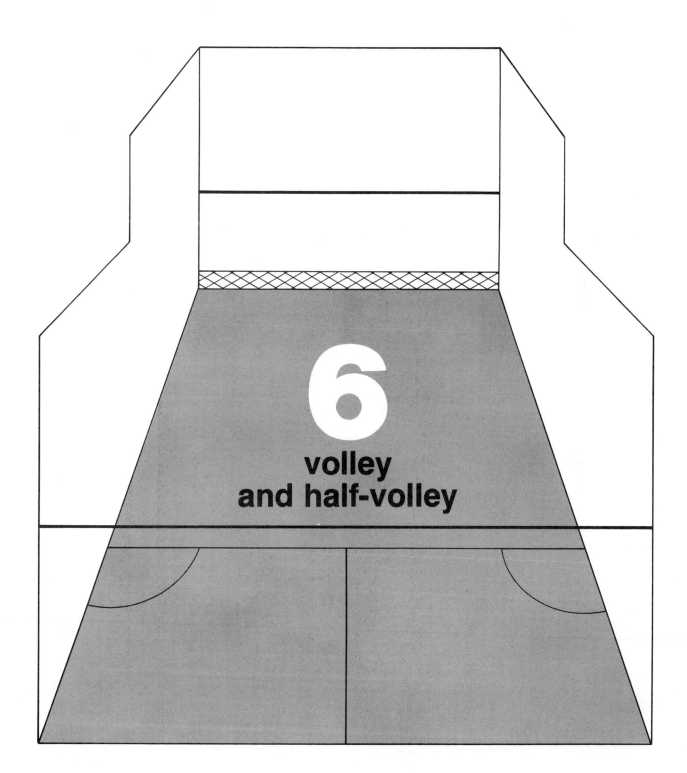

6
volley
and half-volley

VOLLEY

Ground strokes are certainly the bread-and-butter of the game, but the volley provides the topping. An excellent attacking shot, the volley enables the player to speed up the game without hitting the ball any harder. By and large, most volleys will be taken around the short line, demanding quick reflexes, with the ball so often being taken on the wrong foot. This highlights still further the necessity for coaches to instill correct stroke production in the early stages of instruction, as pupils cannot readily handle the wrong-foot ball unless they have been conditioned to take up a balanced stance before stroking.

Executing the Shot

The structure of the body makes it easier to hit a wrong-foot volley on the forehand than on the backhand, but even so, be moving to the ball when making the stroke as this helps to maintain balance. (See Figures 44 and 45.)

The essentials of correct stroking do not change—eyes on the ball, knees bent, wrist cocked and locked, racket head above the wrist, etc.—but the distance of racket travel is restricted. The backswing is much shorter, and the ball is punched rather than being stroked, with the follow-through curtailed. It is imperative therefore, that a tight grip be maintained at the point of impact to ensure

FIGURE 44 Opponent plays a side-wall shot which is too high and out from the wall. I attack with a wrong-foot volley to deny him valuable distance and time, and catch him still moving to the T.

FIGURE 45 Another wrong-foot volley. Opponent played for a drop shot from the back of the court but the shot was far too high. I move quickly, return with a drop shot. Winner. Note that the movement both times is into the ball so as to retain balance.

FIGURE 46. Cross-court volley hit high onto the front wall rebounds onto the side wall and lands behind the opponent.

FIGURE 47 The most difficult shot in squash—the high backhand volley played close to the wall. Very little control is available, so play safe and don't try for a winner.

control—both directional and height above the tin. (See Figure 46.)

As one might expect, a volley played about chest height is easier than one above shoulder level or low down, particularly on the backhand. Somewhat similar to the return of a lob service, the high backhand volley affords the least amount of control and is regarded as probably the most difficult shot, to be played with caution. (See Figure 47.) On the other hand, a high volley on the forehand can be played with more power.

Benefits Resulting from the Use of the Volley

Coaches will find pupils almost without exception, reluctant to play the volley, if for no other reason, through lack of confidence. Acquaint them with the advantages to be gained by taking the ball early, so gaining distance and valuable time. For example, show how a low volley taken at the short line would have become a ground stroke some six feet further back—six feet to the back wall, plus another six feet for the return to an optimum volley position, equals a total of twelve feet. The time for the ball to travel this distance is valuable to both players, so keep this time for yourself and deny it to your opponent. (See Figure 48.)

FIGURE 48 A drop volley counters an opponent's cross-court and is played before he can reach the T. The pace has been taken off the ball with the slice.

Deny your opponent time to get set for a stroke. Bustle him, and if possible make him play a return on the wrong foot. By taking the volley, the player has shortened the distance of ball travel, and by so doing has effectively quickened the pace of the game without varying the speed of the ball.

Volley Practice

Having instructed pupils in playing the volley, the coach must embark on a confidence-building program. I have my pupils stand just behind the short line and volley to their forehand, slowly at first, gradually quickening the pace. Beginners will miss many balls at the start of this exercise, but I tell them not to be overconcerned as my aim is to build their confidence and sharpen their reflexes. Most pupils progress quite rapidly, so after just a couple of sessions, the coach can play to the backhand.

The low volley presents most problems, which invariably result from: (a) not bending the knees, associated with (b) allowing the racket head to fall below the wrist. However, these are by no means the only faults which will cause a poor stroke—all other aspects of correct stroking must be correct. Coaches must stress the advantages of taking the ball as early as possible so as to speed up the tempo of the game and maintain constant pressure on the opponent.

STOP-VOLLEY

This is an effective shot when played at the right time, with accuracy and direction. It is generally more effective if used when an opponent is tiring, rather than early in a match. Allow the ball to hit the racket (using very little swing, but with locked wrist), using its speed and the string tension of the racket to provide the reaction. The head of the racket faces the desired direction, aiming for the front-wall corner, two or three inches above the tin. The shot itself ensures that the speed of the ball is spent when the front wall is struck, causing it to fade on to the side and possibly the nick. (See Figures 49 and 50.)

FIGURE 49 A forehand stop-volley drop shot gains the nick in the right-hand corner.

FIGURE 50 Backhand stop-volley to the backhand corner. Points to note are: racket head above the wrist; open racket face to impart spin; leaning into the ball; eyes are on the ball which has been struck well ahead of the body.

HALF-VOLLEY

A feature of the half-volley is that it is the only stroke in which the ball is struck with the racket head below the wrist. When one considers that it is played so close to the floor, no other wrist/racket combination is possible.

One's *eye* must be good to play the half-volley, and there may be difficulties with stance and balance, but these should not deter the player, for this shot has the advantage, once again, of taking an earlier ball and so pressuring an opponent. (See Figure 51.) The odds against making a half-volley error can be lessened by:

(a) getting down to the ball,

(b) watching it closely, and

(c) not being cramped when making the stroke. (See Figure 52.)

FIGURE 52   The half-volley played correctly, Knees are bent, with the body down as far as possible to the ball, ensuring maximum control and accuracy.

FIGURE 51   G. Hunt (Australia) plays a half-volley against Mohibullah Khan (Pakistan). In this action it is difficult for Hunt to control the ball, playing with the racket in this position and the wrist unlocked. Possible result was the ball hitting the tin, or an easy get for Khan. Even the champions err sometime.

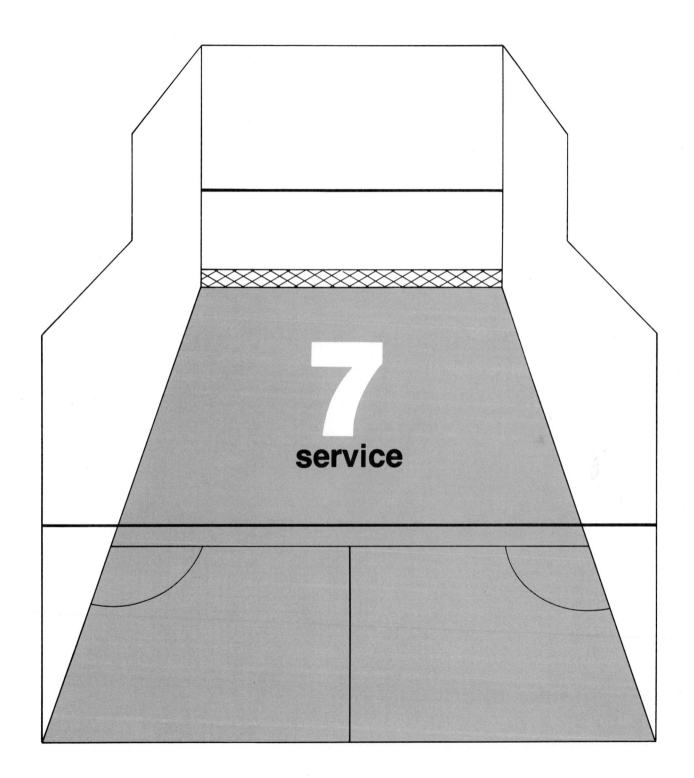

7
service

INTRODUCTION

The service is the only occasion when the player is able to hit a near-stationary ball. This can be a great advantage, so should not be thrown away.

It happens far too often that top-class players take too little care with the service, being simply content to just get the ball into play. When used properly, the service can be a fine attacking weapon, a means of creating an early opening, and/or as a method of breaking an opponent's concentration. The player who thinks and takes care with every service will show a profit for the whole match over the one who does not, and it may be that a well-directed service proves a winner at a vital stage in the game. You have the initiative—keep it.

It is proposed to deal with three types of service—lob, slice, hard—and to treat any other with scant respect.

LOB

Only rarely will your service strike the nick in the back corner and be an outright winner, so you must aim to make the return as difficult as

possible for your opponent, allowing him every opportunity to make a mistake. Shots that pose most problems for players are those close to the wall—where judgement has to be extremely good, the range of shots is limited, and the chances of a mishit are increased.

The lob, when well-directed, will drop sharply, slide off the side wall, and force your opponent to make his stroke near the back wall, as it will be too high for him to reach further forward. The steep descent, plus striking the side wall, takes the pace off the ball, further restricting the bounce to near enough to the back corner to force either an error or a weak defensive return—most likely a boast. Also, do not give him any more *air* around the ball than is necessary, but rather give more wall than he would like. The counter to this and other services is explained in the next chapter.

Service Position and Stance

Throughout the game you must aim to be in a position of command at the T, so hit your service (lob or other type of service), while standing as near to this spot as possible. To achieve this place the right foot where the short line meets the service box, with body weight equally distributed over both feet. As the ball is served the weight is transferred to the left foot in a step to the T enabling the player to be in position for the return with just two short steps. Most times you will be at the T long before your opponent makes his return.

When serving from the right box, the body faces the front wall, and the right side wall when serving from the left. From these positions you have a full view of the court and your opponent, are balanced, and able to be deliberate in your stroke making. By keeping your opponent in view, you are in a position to detect any change in movement or stance he may make. (See Figure 53.)

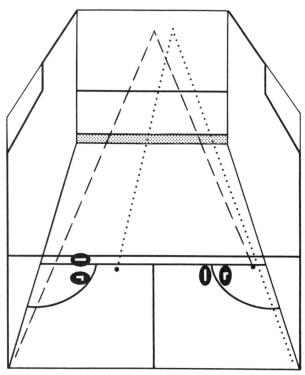

FIGURE 53   Stance and aiming points for the lob service.

Aiming Point

You are endeavoring to slide the ball high off the side wall into the back corner, so where best to hit it on the front wall? The best spot will depend upon the height of the roof, speed of the ball, condition of the walls (be they dry or damp through humidity), and your height. It is for you to make an assessment at the outset of the game, but there is an ideal aiming point. By positioning yourself

nearest the T you have sharpened the angle of attack at which the ball approaches the side wall. To take advantage of this from the right box, strike the ball so that it will hit the front wall on an extended *half-court line* and three-quarters of the way up from the *cut line* to the *out-of-court* line.

From the left box, you will be hitting the ball closer to the T and so have a more acute angle to play with. Once again aim to hit the front wall three-quarters of the way up, but with this narrower angle, aim for a spot about two feet to the right of center and so achieve greater slide along the side wall.

Service Action

Opinions vary as to whether it is better to hit the ball underarm or overhead as in tennis. The constant aim is to keep your opponent guessing; be consistent in body movement and stroke production, and do not introduce any more variables into your game than are necessary. Players serving the lob with an underarm action find it necessary occasionally to vary their action because of a low roof, but if the service action is overhead, there is no need for change. This same action is used for the other services, which will be discussed later.

For the lob, the ball is thrown up a little to the front of the body opposite the right shoulder, and is struck with the arm extended. (See Figures 54 and 55.) Hit from this height, the ball goes through very little angular change in order to meet the ideal spot of three-quarters of the distance up the front wall (approximately 10–11 feet from the floor). This gives a nice downward trajectory into the back corner, reduces the risk of a faulty service below the cut line, and eliminates the worry of hitting the roof. For these obvious reasons, and because of the preponderance of advantages over disadvantages, coaches should discourage pupils from serving with an underarm action. Pupils may initially experience difficulties in changing but perseverance will, in the long run, pay dividends.

Sliced Lob

To aggravate the problem for your opponent, impart slice to the ball when serving.

FIGURE 54   Service action from the right box.

FIGURE 55   Service action from the left box.

From the right box, the ball needs to hit the front wall about one foot to the left of, rather than on the center line, as the spinning action will bring the ball towards the center of the court. However, as you have decreased the angular distance, the slide off the side wall is accentuated.

Serving from the left, the slice takes the ball further to the right after hitting the front wall, causing is to cling to the side wall longer. These small refinements, which are in themselves seemingly insignificant, can be vital in inhibiting an opponent's judgement that small fraction, causing minor loss of control, a mishit or a misdirected shot, and thus open up the court for your attack.

Summary

1. Right foot at the intersection of the service box and the short line.

2. Even balance on both feet.

3. Body facing the front wall when serving from the right box, and side wall when serving from the left.

4. Ball hit above and in front of the right shoulder.

5. Aim to hit the front wall three-quarters of the way up from the cut line and out-of-court line; on the centerline from the right box, and two feet to the right of center from the left.

6. Gain early command of the T.

7. High trajectory.

8. Side wall slide.

9. Back wall fade with little bounce.

10. Restrict opponent to a limited range of shots.

SLICED SERVICE

As with the lob, the sliced service is directed towards the back corner with some slide along the side wall. This is where the use of the overhead action proves so successful—it is the one constant for all services—enabling the player to apply slice, direction and change of pace by the use of slight variations of wrist and arm movement. The action is the same as for the lob, but at the last moment before the racket makes contact with the ball, the wrist is *snapped* through and the racket face *closed* to impart the spin. The ball is hit harder than for the lob, with the aiming point just above the cut line, and about one foot to the left of center when served from the right box (and about two feet at the right of the centerline when served from the left-hand side).

The action of the spin projects the ball along a curved line, relative to the side wall, curving into an opponent receiving on the left,

and away from him on the right side of the court. Imparting spin slows the movement of the ball through the air, both to and from the front wall, but as your service action has remained constant, your opponent will in most cases tend to hit the ball too early, and be cramped on the backhand, and stretched on the forehand. With this service, you have opened the way for a weak or misdirected return which, at a vital stage in a match, may make just that little bit of difference.

Summary

1. Stance and service action are the same as for the lob.

2. At the moment before hitting the ball, close the racket face and flick the wrist through to impart spin.

3. Aim for just above the cut line and one foot to the left of center from the right box, and two feet to the right of the centerline when serving from the left.

4. Curved trajectory, into the opponent receiving on the left, and away from him when standing on the right-hand side of the court.

5. The ball slides off the side wall and into the back corner.

6. The tendency is for the opponent to hit early.

HARD SERVICE

Once again use the same actions for other services, but hit the ball hard and flat, without spin, as you are relying on sheer pace. This service should be used for variety, for a basic change of pace, as a means of breaking an opponent's concentration, and to generally keep him guessing.

It can be directed down the center of the court, off the side wall to rebound into his body, deep into the back corner, or for a direct rebound front wall/back wall. Aim to hit the ball about two feet above the cut line, and in a position relative to the centerline which will achieve a rebound into the desired position.

Potential Dangers

This is a service with inherent dangers for the server, and the coach should make him well aware of the amount of court that will be opened up for an alert opponent. A service down the centerline poses one particular problem, for the server denies himself command of the T. If he does try to take up this position he runs the risk of being hit by the ball and/or racket, suffering both a painful injury and the possible loss of the rally.

CONCLUSIONS

I have discussed three different services, dealing at length with the lob. This is because the lob is the one that gives the player the greatest advantage and initiative at the start of the rally, as well as creating the greatest number of problems for his opponent.

Coaches must advise pupils against using any service other than the lob, except as a surprise weapon to be used to break an opponent's concentration, and to keep him guessing. Used too often, the sliced and hard services lose their surprise value, becoming not only negative but disadvantageous. They should be used sparingly.

Remember, in a long match your opponent will be feeling the effects of fatigue and will find it much more difficult to play the slow service that falls into the back corner than the hard ball down the center of his court.

LEFT-HANDED OPPONENT

Because most players are assumed to have a weaker backhand than forehand, the server generally begins from the right box, giving scant thought to his left-handed opponent. When playing left-handers, commence serving from the left box, for you are not only playing to his assumed weaker side, but are giving him notice of having analyzed his game from the outset. It is another of those minor points that, when added together, win matches.

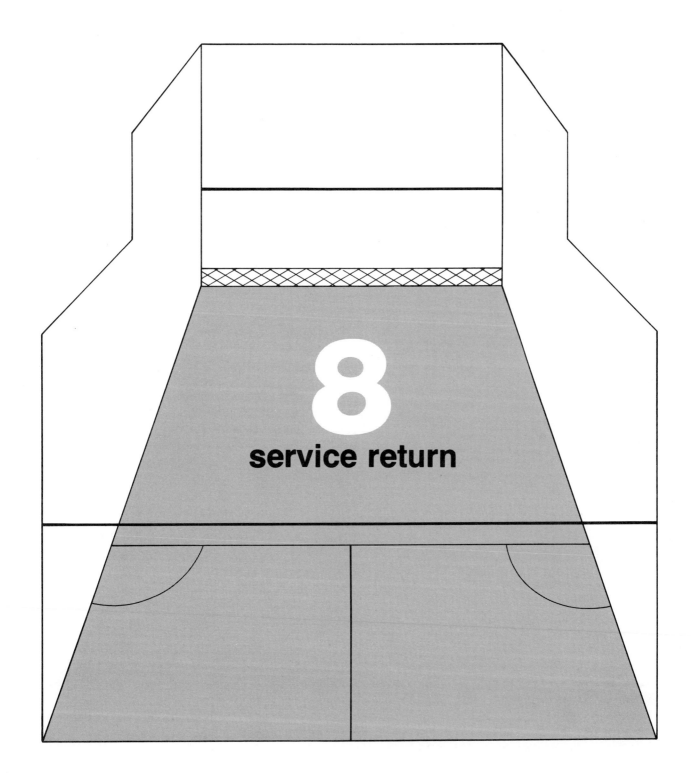

8
service return

INTRODUCTION

In the previous chapter we saw how the server held all the advantages and was able to take the initiative on the first, and possibly most important shot in the rally. Assuming that you have to defend against a good service, the emphasis must be upon taking up a stance that, if not tipping the odds in your favor, does not place you in a more disadvantageous position. Most services received will be directed to the back corner and will force you onto the defensive, so accept any others with thanks and go into the attack.

Your need at all times is for freedom of movement and swing. Give the ball lots of air and don't crowd the service, but be ready to pounce on the short ball, or the one which is further from the side and back walls as the server prefers.

STANCE AND POSITION

The correct stance is one which allows you to watch the server, while at the same time to move with speed, and be in a position to play an effective return. The stance must be balanced and relaxed, yet allow you to spring readily into action, and move rapidly in any direction. The following points should be observed:

1. The feet are spread a comfortable distance apart (optimum is about shoulder width), with the weight evenly distributed, tending to be on the toes rather than the heels.

2. The knees are bent, helping to initiate rapid movement. Avoid standing with stiff legs whenever on the court, for as you will appreciate, it is impossible to move (even to walk) in any direction without first bending the knees.

3. Bend slightly forward to assist balance and anticipated movement.

4. Face the corner where the short line meets the side wall.

5. Take up the stance just inside the half-court line midway between the short line and back wall. (See Figure 56.) From here you have a full view of the court and your opponent (keep your eye on him at all times), and

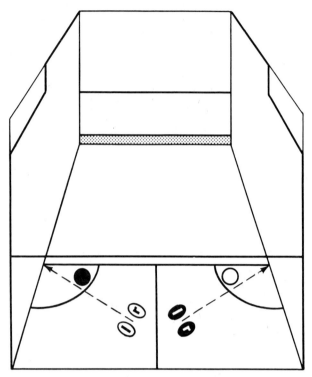

FIGURE 56   Correct positioning of the feet with the player facing the junction of the short line and the side wall.

FIGURE 57   Stance and position when receiving service on the backhand side.

FIGURE 58   Receiving service on the forehand side.

can cover any service with a maximum of just two steps. Even a hard service down the center will not catch you out of position or on the wrong foot, as you are able to merely step aside and play the ball with ease.

6. The racket is held at the ready and not left dangling by the side. To play any shot, the racket head must be above the wrist (half-volley excepted), so be prepared. The squash racket is of light weight and does not need to be cradled in the left hand like a tennis racket. (See Figures 57 and 58.)

PROBLEMS AND SOLUTIONS

As the service gives you the advantage, so the return poses the first problem of the rally. Accepting the fact that most services received will be the lob, the player is confronted with the choice of either striking the falling ball on the volley or waiting for it to bounce. Either way he has a problem, so must make a split-second decision.

Slow-falling Ball

The most effective serve is one which strikes the side wall high and deep, and slides off, having spent most of its speed. The player must decide whether to return before or after the ball strikes the wall, but whatever decision he takes, he will be hitting *across the line* and consequently his judgement must be perfect if his return is to have any authority.

Attempting to take the ball before it strikes the wall, assuming it to be high, causes the player to stretch, and reduces the amount of control he can exercise. But if the ball *is* taken in this position it must be remembered that, not only is it falling, but it is traveling towards the back wall as well, so affording a far greater opportunity for a mistake.

Volley Return

Most of the world's leading players accept that the high backhand volley is the most difficult shot of all. (See Figure 47.) Whenever possible take the ball as it comes off the side wall, playing it opposite the forward knee, which should be slightly bent. (See Figures 59 and 60.) The stroking of this volley (See Chapter 6) does not vary from that made during the rally, but greater care and attention have to be

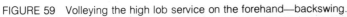

FIGURE 59   Volleying the high lob service on the forehand—backswing.

FIGURE 60   Volleying the high lob service on the backhand—just after point of impact.

taken as the ball will be falling at possibly a steeper angle and a slower pace. (See Figures 61 and 62.)

The decision as to when to play the ball is of vital importance, but the player must avoid allowing the service to bounce on to the floor near the back corner. There it does not have enough speed to rebound very far from the wall and so is either unplayable, or at best, forces a boasted return.

Boasted Return

When confronted with the ball in the back corner, many players go into a mild form of panic, which results in (a) playing a cramped stroke; (b) striking the wall with the racket; (c) getting too close to the ball; or (d) just completely giving up. Possibly the only shot available is the boast, and played correctly, it should hold no fears. But to be suc-

cessful, the following rules must be adhered to:

1. Face the back corner.

2. Lead with the correct leg, towards the corner, as for a normal ground stroke (right leg for the backhand and left leg for the forehand).

3. Keep away from the ball, allowing yourself complete freedom of movement. Remember that it is easier to *fall* those extra few inches into the ball than to lean back. Also, balance is rather difficult to maintain when leaning away from, instead of into, the ball.

4. Play the boast in the normal manner as described in Chapter 5, allowing the swing to turn the body further than normally in

74

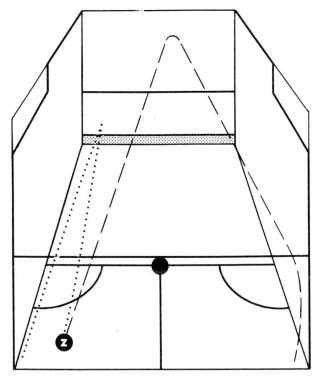

FIGURE 61 The best service return is to a length down the side wall, but for variation play an occasional cross-court lob return in reply. The cross-court lob must be high and must rebound off the opposite side wall to land at the back of the court, by which time it will have lost most of its pace.

order to be facing the opposite front corner upon completion of the follow-through. That is, follow the ball around the corners, and take up a position ahead of the T in anticipation of your opponent's play from the front of the court.

5. The boast can be hit hard or soft, depending on your choice. The softer ball allows the player more time to regain the T position, whereas the harder-played shot may catch an opponent flatfooted.

6. You are going to be at a disadvantage with this shot and must realize that your opponent has a choice of many shots from the front of the court.

HARD SERVICE

Whereas the lob service is slow and demands fine judgment, the hard service is an easier ball to play, but requires faster reflex reaction. Nevertheless, it will be traveling in much the same plane as the racket will be in making the return, so consequently provides a greater margin for accuracy.

FIGURE 62 The lob service to the backhand side has been returned as a lob. Note the good balance, follow-through from the upward stroke which gives height to the ball, and intense concentration as the eyes continue to follow the ball.

THE PROBLEM OF SPEED

Although this service presents its own problems, there are solutions. The main problem will be one of speed, for your opponent will be either testing your reactions or attempting to break your concentration.

Be alert and don't get caught napping! Once you have adopted the correct stance to receive, the hard ball down the center, rather than creating a problem, presents an opportunity for you to go into attack. Simply step back, and playing either a volley or ground stroke, hit the ball hard into the back corner on your side of the court. This prevents the server from advancing to the T. However, should he be foolish enough to try to take up this position, he would run the risk of being hit, or of invoking a *penalty point*. Either way he can lose the rally. The hard service coming off the side wall generally finds its way into the center of the receiver's court, and similarly *stands up* to be played deep down the side wall. Fast reactions, and the need to keep the ball literally at arm's length, are the main essentials for successfully playing the hard service. At no time is this more apparent than when it rebounds off the back wall. It *runs* to the front of the court, so if the receiver does not stay away from the wall, and forward, he will find that the ball has passed his body before the stroke is completed. The coach can demonstrate this very convincingly by playing a hard ball onto the back wall, then showing the effect of: (a) standing too close to the back wall and having the ball run past; and (b) by standing, if anything, too far forward, and away, and showing how the stroke can be made by leaning to the rear in order to play the ball down the wall or boast off the side wall.

SUMMARY

To reduce the margin for error on returning even the best service, it is essential to take up the correct stance and watch your opponent. By watching him you get some advance notice of the type of service to expect.

Having taken every precaution, you must play your return with safety uppermost in your mind. The safest, and most usual return is to a length down the side wall; but on occasions, and generally as a surprise weapon, introduce some variety, bearing in mind the inherent dangers.

The lob service can be returned as a cross-court lob into the opposite corner, and as the server will have moved into the T, this return will constitute an effective attacking shot. However, the return must be high onto the opposite side wall, for if not, you will have presented him with the chance of playing a winner.

Never try to blast a low cross-court return as, more often than not, this will be a loser, not a winner.

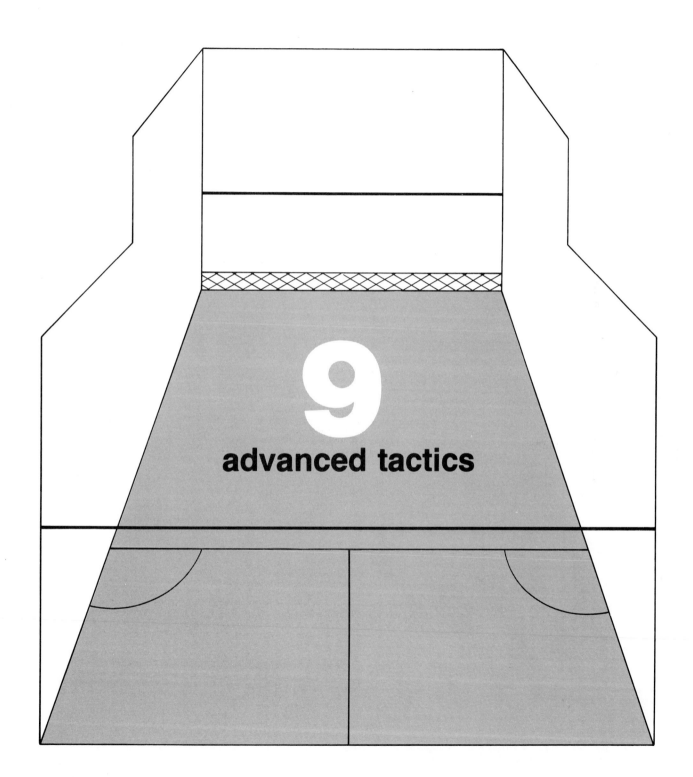

9

advanced tactics

INTRODUCTION

With the world-wide boom that is being experienced in squash, and the subsequent improvement in standards of play, the greater becomes the emphasis on the psychological and physiological aspects of the game. It is assumed always, that the opponent possesses fitness and stamina, and is able to produce the full repertoire of shots.

Tactics, therefore, may well determine the outcome of a match. So, having prepared yourself in the best possible manner, play to a plan, keeping it flexible enough to be varied to suit requirements as the match progresses.

COMMAND OF THE T

The key to tactics must be control of the T, that central position on the court, from which there is the shortest distance to travel to any corner. You must command the T at all times, getting back to this position (within a radius of approximately eighteen inches from the center point) after every shot. If you are to command the T, your opponent must be kept from it, and this is only possible if the ball is kept from rebounding into the center of the court.

Side-wall Drive

The drive to a length down the side wall is the most effective method of drawing your opponent away from the T, and not only presents him with the back-corner problem, but places the ball in the furthest point from the front wall, making an attacking reply that much more difficult.

We once again recognize the importance of the most basic quality of all—control of the ball down the side wall and into the back corner. Simplicity itself; but your opponent, also a good player, will be—or should be—employing the same tactics, being patient, awaiting your mistakes.

Poor Tactics

To draw the opponent away from the T, a cross-court drive may be attempted, but unless played correctly, it will open the way for him to play a winner. The hard-hit low cross-court drive may look spectacular from the gallery but is a poor tactical move. (See Figures 69a and 69b in Chapter 10, "Advanced Shots.") Better to play the ball high and too far away for the volley, so forcing him to play the ball coming in towards his body off the side wall.

Winning Shots from the Front of the Court

Don't be ambitious. Use cross-court shots and boasts from the back of the court sparingly. Apart from those points which are won through the opponent's mistakes, most winning shots come from the front half of the court, so what you must aim for is to:

(a) allow your opponent to commit errors from the back of the court; and

(b) play winners when up front.

By keeping the opponent in the back corners, you are forcing him to defend, as attack is both difficult and rather rash—assuming, of course, that you are watching him and the ball, and not standing at the T staring straight ahead. *Command the T and command the play.*

TACTICAL MOVES

The ideas presented below will help win matches for players who are competing at any level—often when an opponent seems to possess better technical ability.

1. *Prior to a match try to find out all you can about the opponent*—his strengths, weaknesses, fitness, mobility, mannerisms, behavior, etc. You may have played him before, so will have first-hand knowledge. If not, ask those who have, bearing in mind that while not all information may be correct it can be a guide.

2. *Do not confuse warm-up with hit-up.* The two are diametrically opposed and bear no relationship to each other whatsoever. Before going on to the court for the hit-up, a player should warm up and be ready to give 100 percent effort in the first rally of the match.

Climatic conditions vary greatly from country to country and from day to day, but whenever possible before a match, I aim to go for a half-mile run, do twenty knee bends (to the squat position), twenty push-ups, and spend five to ten minutes on a vacant court hitting up. Some of this preparation may not be possible—it may be raining, or there may not be a vacant court—but at least do the push-ups and bends followed by running on the spot for a few minutes. These exercises warm the muscles, preparing them for the activity to follow, and could mean the difference between winning or losing the first few points—which could possibly affect your own and your opponent's psychology for the rest of the match. When you have warmed up, you can walk onto the court for the match happy in the knowledge that you are prepared psychologically and physically as well as possible. But before the match starts there is a hit-up period.

3. *The hit-up is not just a matter of warming the ball,* but is an important learning period during those allowable five minutes before the start of the first game. And this is also the time when your concentration starts. Use this time to analyze your opponent, the shots he plays, the way he moves. Mentally enquire into every aspect. Does he look fit? A thin, wiry player may look fit and could possess stamina, but the one who is fat around the waist and has a large stomach is less likely to sustain any speed and mobility for a five-setter. So keep the rallies long and use up his energy at a faster rate than he would like.

The tall player has to go down further for the low ball, may have more trouble with the drop shot and boast, and may be slow to turn; but for him, the lob and high volley pose fewer problems. The smaller man on the other hand, cannot so easily reach the high ball, but could be fast around the court and play the low ball with comparatively more ease.

Prior to the game you have researched your opponent and built up a mental picture of his strengths and weaknesses. Put this knowledge to the test. Give him a few lobs and see how he copes. He may be effective on the forehand, but balls played to the backhand side may be mishit, or stroked with unease and awkwardness. How does he play the boast (if at all), and has he practiced the drop shot? If he has not taken the trouble to try a few drop shots, backhand and forehand, then perhaps this shot is not strong, in which case he will not give you too much trouble at the front of the court. Note whether he plays any practice shots down the walls, and how he approaches and hits his cross-court shots, once again analyzing both backhand and forehand. Watch your opponent carefully and determine what shots he appears to be protecting, or practicing, and what shots seem to be his favorites.

Irrespective of whether you have had the advantage of an adjacent court for a warm-up session, put the final edge on your shots during the hit-up and try out the full repertoire—length shots, boasts, drops, lobs, cross-courts. Nothing is to be gained from trying to hide your shots from your opponent and it is better to practice and make a few mistakes at this stage when there is nothing to be lost than to try once the match commences. It is too late then to find out that a particular shot is not working.

So often, or more correctly, most often, one sees two players go onto the court for the hit-up and spend the allotted five minutes aimlessly hitting the ball back and forth cross-court to one another. No effort whatsoever is made to practice shots, get the *eye* in, condition the muscles, and get the blood flowing. The time is almost completely wasted and all that is achieved is that the ball gets warm. I utilize the hit-up to the full, practicing not only my shots but taking advantage of the final minute or so to sharpen the reflexes. Throughout play I try to take the ball as early as possible, and to be able to do so I need sharp reflexes. These reflexes are going to be far below peak level if I practice shots only from the back of the court.

To achieve this sharpening process, I stand just forward of the short line during the last minute of the allotted five-minute period, and take whatever ball may come along—a ground stroke, volley, or half-volley. I con-

sider it inconsequential if I mishit a few, for, having practiced the shots during my warm-up and the early minutes of the hit-up, I am concerned only about the reflexes at this stage.

If I have not had the opportunity for a warm-up session on an adjacent court, I must make an assessment, during the hit-up, of conditions and factors that may affect play. Is the court hot or cold? Upon this will depend the speed of the ball. Does it have a high or low roof allowing for or restricting high lobs? Is the roof itself light, or so dark that the lob will become lost in the background? A similar consideration is the floor, which may be constructed of a dark-colored wood, or be discolored. Is the lighting fluorescent or incandescent, opaque or clear (presenting me with the possibility of being "blinded" by the high lob)? And the walls—are they discolored, or dry or sweaty? A damp wall presents its own peculiar problem of causing *slip* for the ball, resulting in the high side-wall shot skidding up into the roof.

4. *Having done the research on your opponent, exploit his weaknesses.* However, be flexible in your approach, being prepared to vary the attack if a weak aspect shows improvement, or to switch to some other play if you find him anticipating too readily.

5. *Do not change a winning formula for experimentation.* Always change tactics if losing, but avoid going into a panic at the loss of a few points. They can be important, but are not necessarily so. Analyze the game. Is your opponent playing to your weakness(es); are you not watching the ball; rushing strokes, etc.? Slow down, take a few deep breaths, THINK. You should be playing the side-wall game, restraining yourself from trying every shot known—but are you? If not, it is a good idea in situations like this, to come right back to the basics. Play down the wall, hit a little higher above the tin, play safe for a few shots, regain your composure and confidence, and then see how the game develops. Do not be in a hurry to win, and above all *don't panic,* for if you do you will most certainly lose.

6. *Control the ball,* hitting it *where* you want, at the *speed* you want. This is the whole basis of the game. Give your opponent every opportunity to make mistakes by either hitting out, missing, or opening the way for you to play a winner.

7. *Play percentage squash.* The player who makes the least number of errors wins the match. Don't go for the winning shot every time you hit the ball. Be patient. By playing the percentage game you do not have to try to win, for by giving your opponent the opening to make a mistake you are allowing him to lose.

8. *Attack is the best form of defense,* but there is a right and wrong time to attack in the generally accepted sense. You should "attack" the ball at all times, for unless you do, the purely defensive shot opens the way for a winner. For example, the shot down the wall may be considered defensive but, if controlled into the back corner, becomes both defense and attack, for you deny your opponent the opportunity to attempt a winner, as he is forced to defend.

Only when the opening presents itself should you go for the pure winner. There are, of course, exceptions to this rule, and I break it myself sometimes, but always with the realization of what I am doing, and of the inherent dangers involved. I may be trying to break an opponent's concentration, or catch him on the wrong foot.

9. *Always move into the ball, be it a ground stroke or volley.* This action is vital if the attacking approach is to be effective. It is rather difficult to attack the ball when playing either from a stance that is too upright or when moving back. Even when playing off the wrong foot, move into the shot, so facilitating balance and follow-through.

10. *The weaker player goes for the winner,* hits the ball well, just where he wanted, then stands back to admire the shot, only to find his opponent get to and play his good shot for a winner. Top-class players never fall into this trap. *Always* assume that your opponent will reach the ball and be in position, and able, to play your good shot for a winner. The rally is only decided when the ball has gone *dead*, and not before.

11. *The best serve is the lob,* but you may face an opponent who is, for example, strong on the forehand high volley and able to direct his return hard down the wall to a length. A change of service is therefore indicated.

Try some serves that come off the wall deep, and into his forehand. But always stick to your basic plan of serving the lob, for you will invariably find that as the match progresses, the shot he played with delight earlier will become ragged and inaccurate as fatigue sets in. His judgement will be off just enough for you to force errors.

12. *Your plan is aimed at allowing him to make the errors.* The game, as it progresses, takes toll of the energy resources of both players, so if you see your opponent's reflexes slowing and his judgement and timing fading, capitalize on this decline in performance. It is sometimes a good idea to hit the ball higher and slower, forcing him to stretch up, this being more demanding than bending down, as he is opposing the force of gravity. Or you may want him to cover more court in retrieving, so try deep cross-court shots, or drops followed by lobs. However, it must be obvious that tactics such as these can only succeed if your own fitness and stamina are beyond question.

13. *Vary the speed of the game.* This can be achieved in a number of ways:

(a) It was demonstrated earlier, when discussing the volley in Chapter 6, that this shot can be employed as a means of speeding up the game without necessarily hitting the ball any harder. By the same token, when playing this shot, the tempo of the game can be slowed down, or quickened still further.

(b) During the rally a certain speed of

ball travel generally develops with both players falling into this groove. The occasional ball hit harder or slower can sometimes impair an opponent's judgement sufficiently to force an error.

(c) For the most part, take the ball early. There are times when it is neither possible nor desirable to do so, but by taking an early ball you are denying your opponent time to move, and that split-second may be the difference between him either attacking, defending, playing a winner, or being forced into error.

(d) A player who hits the ball hard all the time enjoys playing against pace. Don't give him any pace to hit at. Slow the game down, forcing him to play shots. Conversely, there is the one who plays slow balls. He should be bustled and made to chase fast balls around the court.

14. *The previous rally is history,* and win or lose, there is nothing you can do about it, so get on with the game. If you have won, you won't have any worries; and worrying is not going to help if you have lost. But analyze the rally, determine what went wrong, and learn from either your mistake or your opponent's good play. Take corrective action in the next rally.

15. *Good behavior on the court* is rarely mentioned, being accepted as normal—and so it should be. Go into a game to win, give of your best, and having done so and been beaten, congratulate your opponent. There is no place in the game for bad behavior, which thankfully is confined to a narrow fringe who do the game no good, but who do get the questionable publicity.

Allowance is made in the rules for appeal to the referee. If an appeal is made, accept the decision and carry on with the game even though you may not agree. The referee rules on play as he sees it, acting as an impartial arbitrator.

There will be players who deliberately set out to irrate in the hope of destroying their opponent's concentration. Ignore them and concentrate on your game.

16. *Keep your eyes on the ball,* and a close watch on your opponent. A fatal mistake is to stand at the T staring straight ahead as if wearing a pair of blinkers. In this position you have no idea what your opponent is doing, or where the ball is going until it goes past you. If your timing has gone off, or you are playing badly, *concentrate*, making a conscious effort to watch the ball very closely.

17. *Command the T at all times.* This can only be done if you deny it to your opponent with shots down the side walls or into the corners. Depending on your opponent's position on the court during the rally, vary your own position at the T within a radius of eighteen inches from the center point.

18. *Keep the knees bent at all times,* and remain alert and in a crouched position, ready to move quickly in any direction.

19. *Take large steps when moving into a shot,* using shuffling steps for the final adjustment of position prior to hitting the ball.

20. *Patience is the virtue that should be exercised throughout the game,* as you wait for the right ball to come along to be hit for a winner, or until your opponent either makes an error or fails to retrieve your shot.

21. *Never allow yourself to get into a position on the court where you have to turn to make good the return.* It is bad play, losing distance, time, and possibly sight of the ball. If an opponent turns, get out of the way of his return and lose the rally rather than get hit by the ball.

22. *With the best will in the world accidents happen* in which a player gets hit by racket or ball. Be conscious that this is a possibility and always stop if you think that, in playing a certain shot, you may strike an opponent. In friendly games your opponent will give a *let,* and in competition the referee will exercise his

discretion and allow the let for genuine appeals.

23. *Most people are right-handed* and adopt a pattern of play accordingly, hitting mostly to the backhand side, hoping for an added advantage. When playing left-handers, tactics must be varied; for example, start the serve from the left, and play more to the right court. Be aware right from the hit-up that your opponent is left-handed. I have so often seen players lose the first game without realizing that their opponent was left-handed. Don't be caught napping!

24. *It is of little use, besides being poor percentage squash, to play too many lobs and drops on a fast court with a low ceiling.* Equally, it is useless to hit the ball hard all the time on a cold court against an opponent who possesses a fine drop shot. Adapt your game to counter your opponent's play and the state of the court.

25. *Play a spoiling game against your opponent* and try to impose upon him the type of game that suits you. If your game is basically a slow one, your best tactic is to keep your opponent in the back corners until the ball is presented in the front half of the court, then play an accurate drop shot. Or if you have been caught by an alert opponent who rushes up to counter the drop shot, play a hard shot to a length down the wall, or cross-court.

26. *The start of the game is when errors are likely through nerves*, if at all, and through players going for winners too soon rather than adjusting to the speed of the game, and ball, which will be greater than at the hit-up. Get into the game gradually, playing with some caution and let your opponent try for the early winner, with you giving him every chance to make a mistake.

27. *Having gained an early ascendency, be a little more daring* and, given the opening, try some of your favorite shots that could build up the lead. If they fail and your lead is reduced,

once again play a safe accurate type of game and regain the lead and your confidence, by which time you may have won the first game easily.

28. *Do not squander your one-minute break between games* (two minutes between the fourth and fifth games) by trying to do so many things which may be considered unnecessary, like combing the hair, drinking water, or talking to club members. If you are interested in breaking your concentration, then go ahead, but I do not recommend it, as you will start the next set as tired as at the end of the last. I never leave the court between games, preferring to wander around the arena collecting my thoughts, thinking about what has gone before; deciding what I can do to maintain my winning streak, or contemplating changes to counter my opponent's good form and get back into the game. By standing around outside the court one is liable to get stiff and so be at a disadvantage at the start of the next game, maybe losing those first few vital points. In addition, the lighting outside is dimmer than on the court, and the eyes have to adjust at the start of a new game.

Playing in hot humid conditions such as one finds in the tropics, will mean that you sweat a lot and will welcome the chance to towel down during the break. It is a good idea to leave a towel with a spectator in the gallery, and retrieve it at the end of each game, to give yourself a rub-down as you walk around the court.

29. *Approach each game as you approached the preceding one*—with caution—and once again try to take an early lead. But how little thought is given to the fact that while the players have been cooling off for one minute, so has the ball, and that the tactics that worked at the start of the first game may not necessarily work at the start of the second, or subsequent games.

The lob service that put the opponent under great pressure at the start of the match will not be so deep at the commencement of the second game, and may present him with the opportunity to attack the very first ball he receives. So think about hitting the ball just a little harder on service to get the same depth from it as you did when it was warm. By the same token, as the receiver, you should be aware that the ball will not travel at the same speed and will take a few shots to reach its optimum playing temperature.

30. *You must discount the possibility of being allowed to take an early lead in every game but,* if this does happen, do not throw away the advantage by attempting (unnecessary) risky winners. Nor is it likely that you will get into a desperate situation where you go for the killing shot all the time, or, at the other end of the spectrum, retrieve and defend on every shot without trying a winner.

Long rallies, a slow-moving score, ever-increasing demands on your energy resources and stamina, coupled with increasing fatigue, place further doubts in your mind as to whether the plan you are adopting is the correct one, and should be continued, or whether a change is indicated. One cannot be specific under these circumstances but your concentration must not be allowed to lapse, and tired as you may become, thinking and planning must continue. Remember, if you are getting tired, so possibly is your opponent, and if you are watching him closely you will have a fair indication of his condition. But don't be lulled into a sense of false security by an opponent who feigns exhaustion. He may be bluffing.

One of the best exponents of this tactic was a good friend of mine, Nick Ingram, against whom I played many times both socially and competitively during the years we lived in Singapore and Malaysia. At the end of each and every game, be it the first or fourth, Nick would give the impression by words and deeds that he was ready for a massive rescue operation by a medical team, protesting that he was only commencing the next game as a matter of conscience. He would then proceed to run as never before.

Possibly try an increase in speed and length of the rallies; put up a few high lobs to make your opponent stretch; or some hard cross-court shots to the corners. Keep him guessing, and if he misses the odd shot and appears apprehensive about playing it, give him a few more and watch his reaction.

31. *Having prepared yourself physically for the match* and being happy in the knowledge that your stamina is better than your opponent's, you should continue with the plan of being in no hurry to win. With your opponent showing some signs of fatigue, it is to your advantage to make the next few rallies long and fast, mixed with drop shots and deep back-corner lobs, and not go for the outright winner. The winners may work and win the odd point or two, but the rallies could be short, enabling him to get his breath and recover somewhat. Longer rallies will aggravate his fatigue, enabling you to play future shots with less risk.

32. *There is much that can be said about the let* and during a match, appeals should be directed to the referee: he makes the decision. However, it is worthwhile discussing the subject here and clarifying a few points.

One must realize that any number of attempts can be made to hit the ball but, if an attempt has been made, one is not allowed to claim, nor is the referee permitted to grant a let. Obviously, this rule is just, for if the shot had gone for a winner, the player would not ask for a let, so you can't have it both ways.

The rules governing the let state that a player must give his opponent complete freedom of strike, the player being free to play any shot he chooses. However, if he finds that he cannot play the shot he originally intended for fear of hitting his opponent with the ball, whether the latter is in a direct line with the front wall, or if the ball would have struck another wall first (in both cases the return would have been good), the player should not feel obliged to play an alternative shot which may have been a loser, or present his opponent with an opening for a winner. In other words, the striker of the ball must have complete freedom to choose whatever shot he wishes and, if unable to do so, is entitled to a let. However, under these circumstances the choice of claiming the let or playing any other shot is his. Having this choice, it may be to your advantage to play another shot and keep the rally going if your opponent is getting tired, rather than let him have a breather before restarting the rally.

Other situations may arise where an opponent obstructs simply by being off-balance and when almost any shot you play will be a winner. It is to your advantage to play the ball. But if you play, or play at, the ball, a let will not be allowed if it subsequently goes out, irrespective of whether the opponent obstructs or not.

Situations will occur during a match where doubts will arise in your mind as to whether an opponent has made a get or whether the ball has landed out of court. If this happens, continue the rally to a conclusion, then, and only then, make your appeal to the referee. You certainly will not appeal if you win the rally. Referees make mistakes—which is only human—but having made your appeal and having had it turned down, accept the decision and get on with the game.

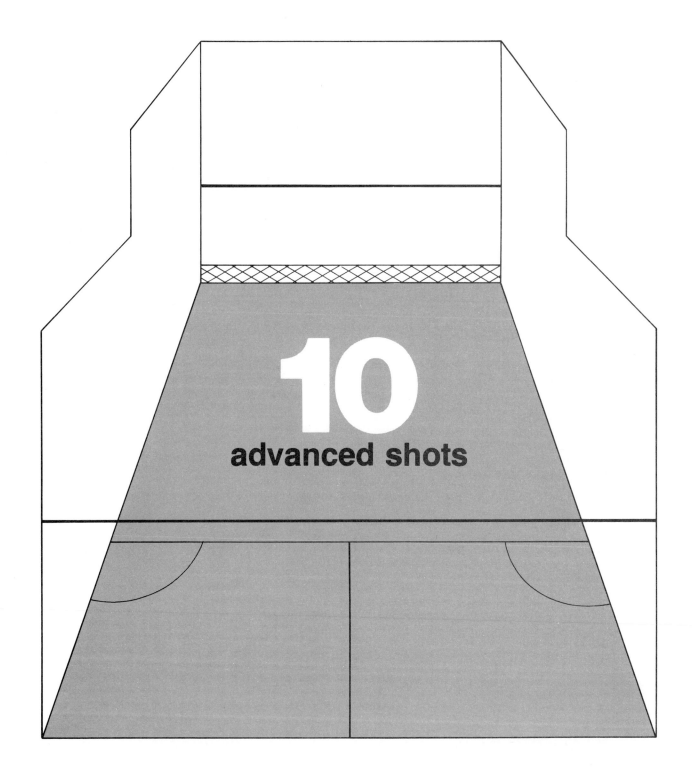

10
advanced shots

TYPICAL SITUATIONS AND SOLUTIONS

There are no new shots in squash and I don't claim any. All of the top players have a full range of shots, and are capable of producing them when not under pressure, but the winner of the rally, and match, is the player who can play the right shot at the right time during conditions of physical and mental stress. Some of the situations in which you may find yourself, and solutions to these problems, are illustrated in the diagrams which follow. This is merely a selection of typical situations, for it would be quite impossible to reproduce every possibility.

Situation
I elect to go cross-court rather than down the wall but the ball is too low on the front wall (Figure 63a).

Opponent, from a good T position gets to the ball and easily plays a drop shot. His shot is poor, too far from the side wall so it cannot *fade* or get the nick (Figure 63b).

He follows me, and rather than play a drop in reply, I send the ball hard onto front,

side walls, and it finishes in the back center of the court (Figure 63c).

FIGURE 63a.

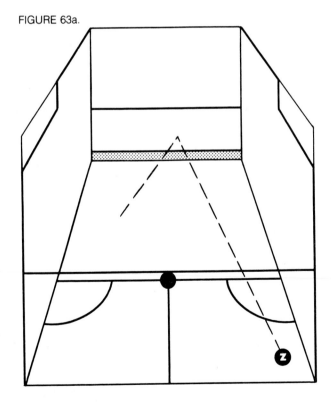

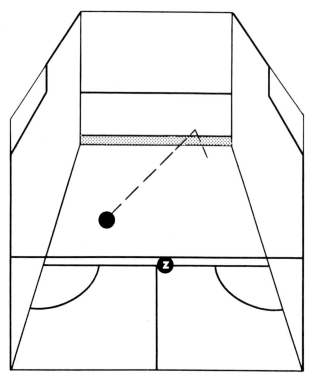

FIGURE 63b.

FIGURE 63c.

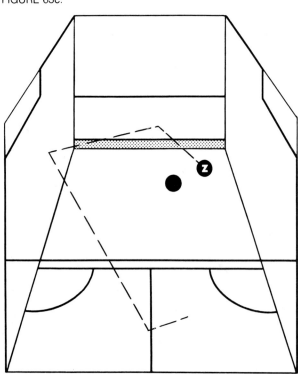

Situation

Opponent's shot lands in the front, backhand corner. Many alternative shots are available to me, and depending upon his position on the court—besides pursuing my continuous aim of keeping him guessing—I play the shot which I consider best under the circumstances. Four alternatives (Figure 64) are:

1. the boast

2. drop shot or hard kill into the nick

3. cross-court drop shot

4. reverse boast.

Situation

Opponent serves a lob, or sends a high return to the backhand, but the ball does not come back far enough or close to the wall (Figure 65a).

I take the ball above shoulder height, hit it hard with heavy slice, 2–3 inches above the tin onto the right front wall and about one foot from the side wall (Figure 65b). Hit to the correct spot on the front wall, with the slide, it dies in the nick. While this is my favorite shot, I recognize its many built-in dangers and play it sparingly, for if it is too low, I hit the tin; too high, and my opponent has a chance for a winner.

Situation

The serve is hard and I decide against the volley, preferring to let the ball strike the back wall and bounce back to the center (Figure 66a).

Opponent does not get a back-wall nick; the ball is too far out from the corner and the rebound gives me an opening to play a hard drive to a length into the backhand corner (Figure 66b).

Situation

A lob played by the opponent is too high to volley so I am forced into the back of the court (Figure 67a). The lob would have been better if closer to the side wall.

I wait for the ball to bounce off the back wall, then play a hard boast, aiming for a

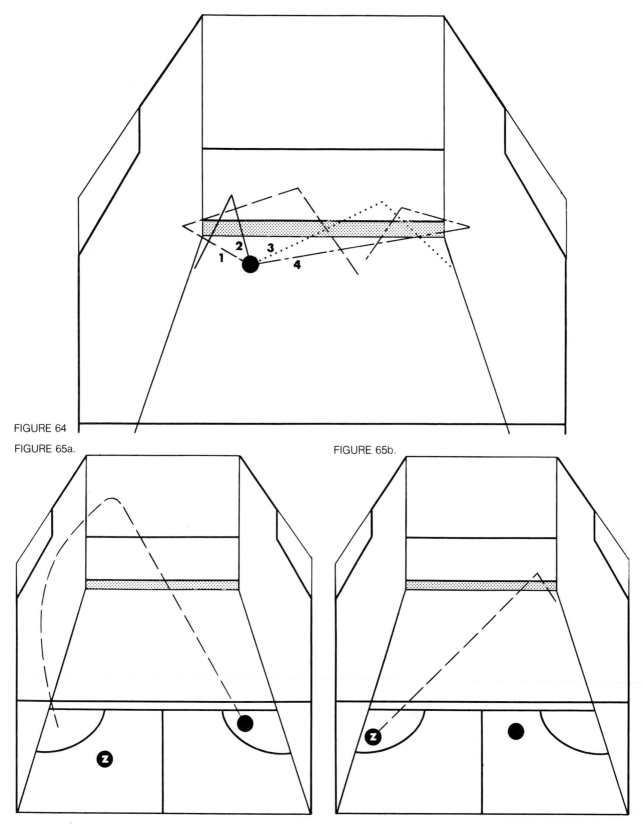

FIGURE 64

FIGURE 65a.

FIGURE 65b.

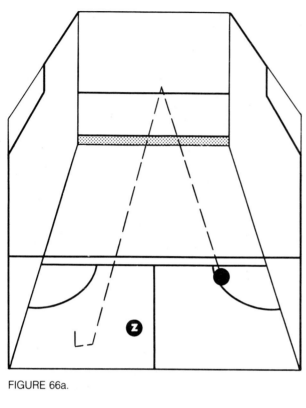

FIGURE 66a.

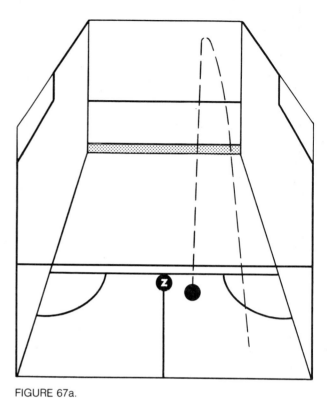

FIGURE 67a.

FIGURE 66b.

FIGURE 67b.

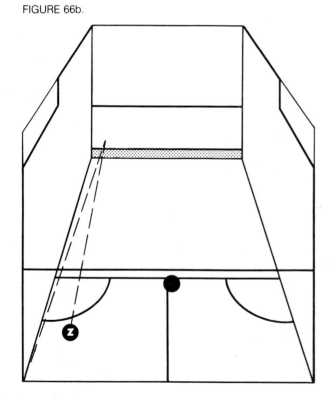

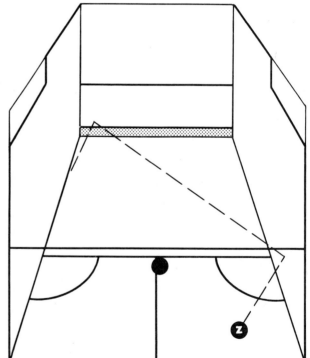

side-wall nick (Figure 67b). Opponent easily gets this shot unless the ball strikes the nick.

Situation

Opponent plays cross-court to the back-hand corner but the ball is too high above the tin and lands back and out from the side wall (Figure 68a).

From the T, I have plenty of time to see this shot, and run quickly and play a drop shot (Figure 68b). Remember, the good drop shot is front wall, side wall, with the ball dying in the nick.

Situation

Opponent hopes to catch me with a cross-court and may have achieved his objective, but he hit the ball too low and close to the centerline (Figure 69a).

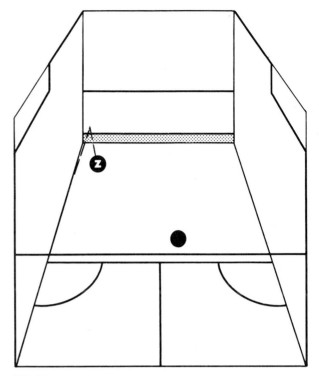

FIGURE 68b.

FIGURE 68a.

FIGURE 69a.

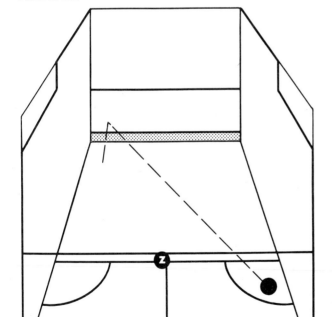

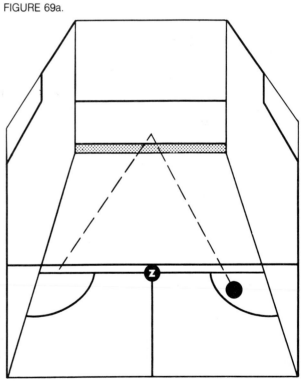

From the T, I get the ball in two steps and decide to match surprise with surprise by playing a reverse boast rather than to a length down the side wall, or a drop shot (Figure 69b).

Situation

From the backhand, just behind the short line, the opponent goes cross-court, but the shot has a bad angle, is too low, and lands forward of the T, which I command (Figure 70a).

With little distance to move I have plenty of time, playing a hard sliced forehand to the front backhand nick (Figure 70b).

Situation

Opponent plays a good drop shot, as a surprise, off the backhand from near the center of the court (Figure 71a).

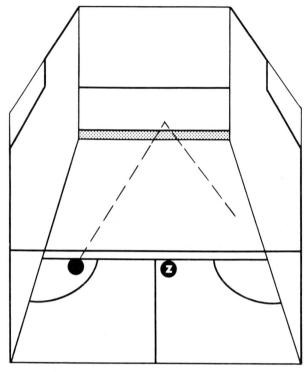

FIGURE 70a.

FIGURE 69b.

FIGURE 70b.

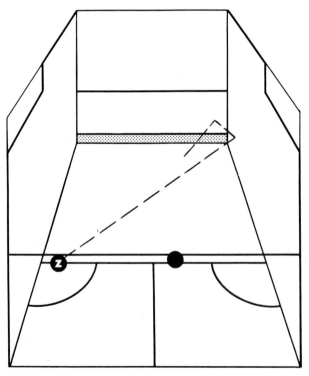

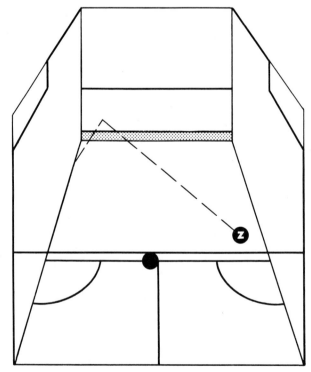

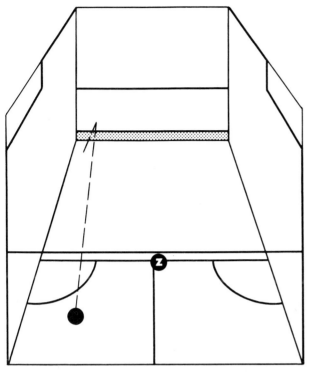

FIGURE 71a.

I react slowly so have to rush to make a get. I reach the ball but am at full stretch so it is dangerous to try a winner or attacking shot (Figure 71b). Best to play a lob back down the wall, or cross-court with the ball hitting high on the front wall, side wall, finishing in the rear center court. Then move to the T, being content to attack later.

Situation

Opponent's lob service drops short of the backhand corner (Figure 72a).

To keep him guessing, I return with a lob volley cross-court to the forehand corner and move to the T (Figure 72b).

He would have been well advised to play down the wall but hits cross-court. The angle is bad, the ball too low and slow (Figure 72c).

I move quickly and play a drop shot (Figure 72d).

FIGURE 71b.

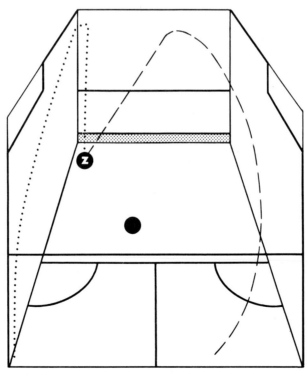

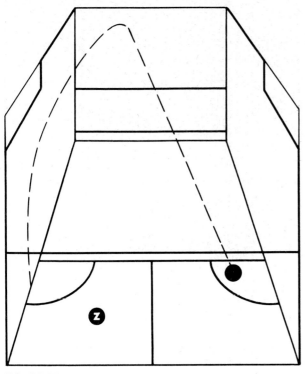

FIGURE 72a.

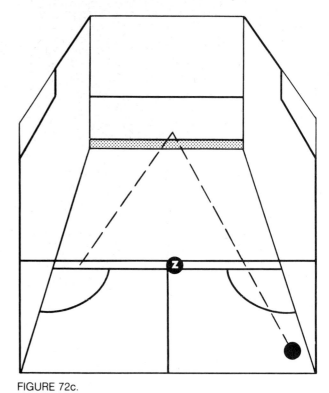

FIGURE 72c.

FIGURE 72b.

FIGURE 72d.

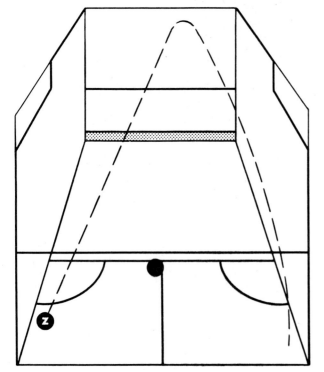

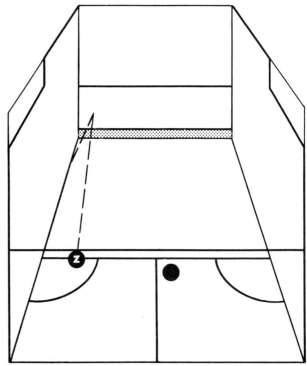

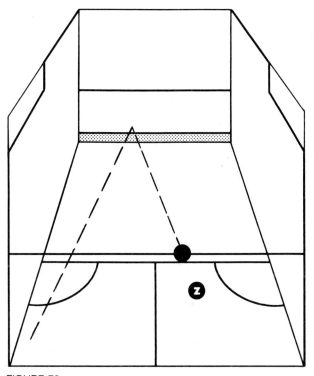

FIGURE 73a.

FIGURE 73b.

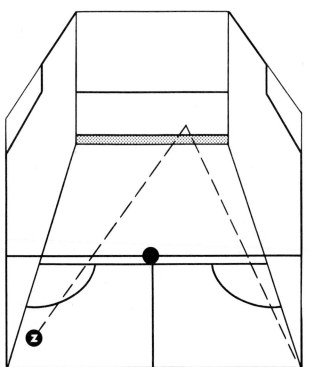

Situation

My return was poor, coming back to my opponent at the T, so I am in trouble. He is in a position to play any shot of his choice but elects a backhand to the back corner (Figure 73a). I am grateful.

I move quickly and play my second most favorite shot—a heavy sliced backhand—cross-court, 2–3 inches above the tin (Figure 73b). The ball stays low and fades into the back corner.

11

fitness training

THERE IS NO EASY WAY
TO FITNESS

Following ball control, fitness and stamina were listed as the next most important qualities of a good squash player. Most people play the game to keep fit, and there can be no argument with this approach, but to play competitively and vie for top place in the sport, one must train, and train hard, both on and off the court. Nobody is naturally fit. Good condition can only come through dedication and a lot of hard work. There is no easy way. But if the correct training program is adopted, and is strictly adhered to, the physical benefits that will accrue will far outweigh all other considerations.

To play good squash one needs both speed and stamina; it is pointless having one without the other. Get your speed from playing and stamina from training off the court. Stamina allows you to play a waiting game and be patient, but if your condition is suspect, you will be inclined to go for winners more often than you should, possibly allowing your opponent to steal the initiative.

Over the years I have developed a training regimen that I find to be the most suitable, and although it is the one I recommend, there may be certain aspects which can be altered, or added to for individual needs.

When a certain level of fitness has been achieved you should try and retain it. Training then feels gradually easier. Less training is required to retain good physical condition than to acquire it. That's why regularity is so important. If you begin your "shake-up" by training every day or every other day for a few weeks, you can achieve good results which can be preserved without much effort. . . .

The author gratefully acknowledges permission from the following sources to reproduce the material quoted in this chapter: [1 and 3] Professor Per-Olof Astrand, *Health and Fitness* (Skandia Insurance Company Limited, Stockholm, 1973); [2] Kenneth H. Cooper, *The New Aerobics* (Bantam Books Inc., New York, 1970); [4] J. V. G. A. Durnin and R. Passmore, *Energy, Work and Leisure* (Heinemann Education Books Ltd., London, 1967); [5] C. S. Leithead and R. A. Lind, *Heat Stress and Heat Disorders* (Cassell and Collier Macmillan Publishers Ltd., London, 1964); [6] Dr. David C. Reid, The University of Alberta, Canada; [7] Professor Per-Olof Astrand and Karl Rodahl, *Textbook of Work Physiology* (McGraw-Hill Book Company, New York, 1970); [8] *Journal of the American Medical Association*.

One important aim of regular physical training is to achieve a physical condition and fitness that is well above that required for the routine job. If daily work forces the heart to pump ten liters of blood/min with a 120 beat/min heart rate, it is obviously advantageous for a person to be trained for 15 liters/min and a 150 beat/min heart rate or more. In view of this, a quick walk now and again may be sufficient for a teacher or office worker, but a person who does heavy work should exercise harder a few sessions a week. [1].

(Refer to the recommended training program discussed later in this chapter.)

AGE IS NO BARRIER TO FITNESS

By all means modify training programs to allow for age, sex, degree of fitness at the start of a program, level of fitness aimed for, etc. For children, I do not seek to lay down hard and fast rules for training, but coaches should make them aware of the need to be fit. This awareness constitutes conditioning more of a psychological than physiological nature, as they get lots of exercise through their youthful exuberance. Age is not an obstacle to fitness. No matter what age bracket you belong to, you can reach a satisfactory level of fitness, but you must work toward the common goal using a different approach, and at a different rate.

One needs to know not only how to get fit but how fitness relates to performance—what physical changes one can expect during a match—appreciating that whatever factors are affecting one player are having the same effect on the other. This knowledge can help a player to aggravate his opponent's fatigue. The fit player will, over a long match, always beat his opponent who may even be a little better technically. I have drawn upon my experience, as well as that of others eminently qualified in the fields of sports medicine and physiology to show how such matters as heat, sweat, stress, etc., can affect the body under conditions of strenuous activity; how training can help lessen the effects; how performance can be increased with this knowledge; what safeguards can be taken to avoid muscle injury; and what benefits can be achieved through diet.

AEROBIC CAPACITY

The maximum amount of oxygen that the body can process within a given time is called the *aerobic capacity*. It is dependent upon an ability to:

1. rapidly breathe large amounts of air;

2. forcefully deliver large volumes of blood; and

3. effectively deliver oxygen to all parts of the body.

Collectively, it depends upon efficient lungs, a powerful heart, and a good vascular system. Because it reflects the condition of these vital organs, the aerobic capacity is the best indicator of physical fitness.

Collectively, the change induced by exercise in the various systems and organs of the body is called the *training effect,* but to be effective, exercise must be of sufficient intensity and duration. You achieve a greater training effect if you put more effort into your exercise.

Sound training increases the capacity to utilize oxygen in several ways:

1. It strengthens the muscles of respiration and tends to reduce the resistance to airflow, ultimately facilitating the rapid flow of air in and out of the lungs.

2. It improves the strength and pumping efficiency of the heart, enabling more blood to be pumped with each stroke. This improves the ability to more rapidly transport oxygen from the lungs to the heart and ultimately to all parts of the body.

3. It tones up muscles throughout the body, thereby improving the general circulation, at times lowering blood pressure and reducing the work on the heart. (See Figure 74.)

4. It causes an increase in the total amount of blood circulating through the body, and increases the number of red blood cells and the amount of hemoglobin, making the blood a more effective oxygen carrier. [2]

Studies have proved that we, with regular training, can counteract (if not completely prevent!) the decline in maximum motor power which usually accompanies increasing age beyond 20. We could put it this way: if two 50-year-olds are identical in endowment but one is trained and the other untrained, then the trained person would have an oxygen uptake ability (and maximum motor power) on the same level as the untrained person had around the age of 35–40. In other words, moderate training can lead to a 10–15 year biological rejuvenation in this respect. [3]

A fit, trained athlete can perform for short periods which involve the utilization of oxygen at the rate of 4 to 5 liters/minute which is 16 to 20 times the resting rate. . . .

Oxygen Debt When the body is working at these high rates, the oxygen supply to the tissues is insufficient to allow the complete oxidation of carbohydrate. Energy is provided by the anaerobic conversion of glucose into lactic acid. Lactic acid accumulates in the tissues. It is removed subsequently by oxidation during the recovery period. Severe exercise is always followed by a period of panting, when the respiration is much above the resting level. This extra oxygen uptake after exercise is known as the oxygen debt. After . . . [a hard game] a fit man may run up an oxygen debt of up to 4 liters. Most of this is used to oxidize lactic acid.

FIGURE 74   Heart-rate after approximately five minutes on a bicycle ergometer (load 150 watts) in conjunction with three months of training. Note that the heart rate gradually declines thanks to training of the heart. (Illustrated by courtesy of Health and Fitness.)

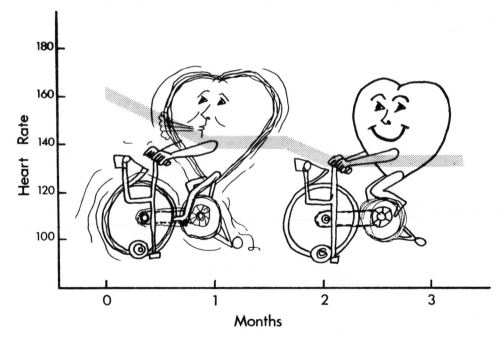

The upper level of work at which glucose is utilized completely and at which no oxygen debt accumulates in the body is [this] aerobic capacity. At this level the circulation can provide the working muscles immediately with all the oxygen they need. . . . The higher the degree of physical fitness the higher the aerobic capacity. . . .

Fatigue If a man works at a constant rate within his aerobic capacity, he reaches after 2 to 4 minutes what physiologists call a *steady state*. This means that he can continue working at this rate for a long period (at least 2 to 3 hours) with a steady heart rate and a steady pulmonary ventilation rate and with no rise in the blood lactic acid. The body temperature rises slowly, perhaps for 30 min, but then also becomes steady—1 to 2° C. above the normal level. When exercise ceases, the pulse rate and ventilation rapidly return to the resting levels—within 2 to 3 min: the oxygen debt is very small, less than one liter. He is not fatigued. . . .

[If a player's] aerobic capacity [is exceeded] the heart rate, pulmonary ventilation, blood lactic acid and body temperature continue to rise throughout the . . . [game at a proportionate rate]. The [player] becomes fatigued and there is a limit to the time during which he can [play]. When [play] ceases, there is a long period of recovery before these values return to resting levels. After very severe exercise, the recovery period may be one hour or even longer. [4]

Bodily Heat Production The amount of heat generated in the body as a result of metabolic activity may vary greatly. . . .

It is seldom appreciated that merely moderate rates of energy expenditure involve the body in the continuous dissipation of large quantities of heat. Even at rest the body produces enough heat to raise the temperature of all its tissues by approximately 1° C./hr. (1.8° F./hr.) if this heat were not dissipated, while an average energy expenditure of 300 cal./hr. would, in the event of the failure of the body to dissipate any heat, raise body temperature by about 5° C./hr. (9° F./hr.). It is an eloquent comment on the efficiency of the thermoregulatory system that these quantities of heat can be easily dissipated, even in climates in which there are additional heat gains by convection or radiation.

Evaporation Sweat produced on to the surface of the skin evaporates when the vapor pressure on the skin is higher than the vapor pressure in the surrounding atmosphere. . . . The evaporation of sweat is the body's principal method of dissipating heat in hot climates; the evaporation of one liter (1.7 imperial pints) of sweat from the skin represents the loss of heat from the body of about 600 cal. (2380 Btu).

The determination of heat lost by sweating is more complicated than heat exchanges by other channels. The present concept is that as the demand increases for heat loss by evaporation, the amount of sweat produced is associated with the increase of the amount of the skin that is wetted. Eventually the whole surface area of the skin is wetted, and further increases of sweat production result in no further benefit to the body as a means of losing heat, since the excess sweat drips from the skin and is not evaporated on it. . . . [5]

DRINKING DURING A GAME

On an average one can expect to burn up 600–900 cal. and sweat 1–1½ liters during an hour-long hard game on a hot humid day. It is important that this water be replaced but it is inadvisable to take any more than a few sips during the game as no benefit can be gained. The gut cannot process the water fast enough

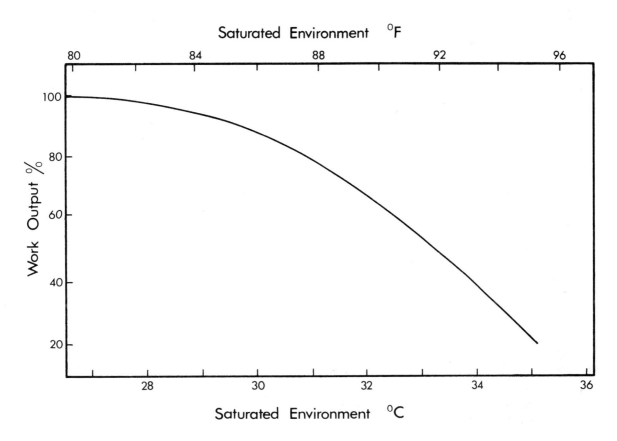

FIGURE 75   The work output of South African gold-miners filling mine cars in a variety of heated environments (Illustration by courtesy of Heat Stress and Heat Disorders).

to have any real effect. An indication of the decrease in ability to perform under hot/humid conditions can be gauged from Figure 75.

When replacing the fluid after a game the optimal temperature is about 50–60 degrees F. Warmer fluids will not help to dissipate that heat, colder fluids could cause some stomach cramp or discomfort. Remember, *humans cannot be taught to adjust to decreased water intake.* Sweat is composed essentially of water and salt. The body maintains a natural balance between the two and a supplement of salt tablets is as inadvisable as it is unnecessary, for the end result would be a change in balance, with the body demanding more water to compensate. A normal diet contains enough salt.

Potassium Supplementation There have been many recent reports that indicate that potassium supplementation may

be as important as simple salt replacement in athletes who are working out under extremely hot conditions. . . .

Considerable potassium is lost in perspiration and the critical levels of 2.5 to 4.5 m.eq. per liter of plasma must be maintained. The mineral and its electrolyte are essential for the optimal functioning of muscle and muscle contraction, both skeletal and cardiac. It plays a key role in maintaining osmotic pressure and water balance between the body fluids and cells. Low levels of potassium may lead to weakness, fatigue, poor intestinal tone, cardiac arrythmias and alteration in respiratory and kidney function.

It is generally felt that most individuals get enough potassium in their ordinary diet and the athlete is no exception providing he gets the right foods. Particularly good natural sources of potassium are tomato juice and bananas. A large banana contains 740 milligrams of potassium. In addition, bran, whole grain bread, cereals, fish, legumes, nuts, and meat all contain good quantities of potassium.

Despite this, hard training athletes, working in hot indoor or out-door conditions for long periods may be well advised to take supplementation in the form of tablets, or even just extra tomato juice. [6]

ENERGY SOURCE

Whenever muscles are brought into play, the energy required for motivation comes through the transformation of glycogen (stored in the muscles) into glucose.

In Sweden an experiment was conducted using nine athletes who

spent 3 days on an extreme fat and protein diet, the glycogen concentration was reduced to about 0.6 g/100 g wet muscle and the standard load could only be performed for about 60 min. After 3 days on a carbohydrate-rich diet, the subjects' glycogen content became higher, 3.5 g/100 g wet muscle, and the time on the 75 percent maximal oxygen uptake could now be prolonged to about 170 min. (average figures).

It was further observed that the most pronounced effect was obtained if the glycogen depots were first emptied by heavy prolonged exercise and then maintained low by giving the subject a diet low in carbohydrate, followed by a few days with a diet rich in carbohydrates. With this procedure the glycogen content could exceed 4 g/100 g wet muscle and the heavy load could be tolerated for longer periods, in some subjects for more than 4 hrs. The total muscle glycogen content under these conditions could exceed 700 g.

Figure 76 illustrates an experiment in

which one subject worked with his left leg and the other subject simultaneously worked with his right leg on the same bicycle ergometer. After several hours' work the exercising leg was emptied of glycogen while the resting leg still had a normal glycogen content. It should be recalled that there are no enzymes present in the skeletal muscles that can transform glycogen to glucose.... Feeding the subjects carbohydrate-rich diet the following days did not markedly influence the depots of the resting limb, but in the previously exercised leg the glycogen content increased rapidly until the values were about twice as high as those in the nonexercised leg. Again, exercise with glycogen depletion enhances the resynthesis of glycogen and the factor (presently unknown) must be operating locally in the exercising muscle....

We may, therefore, conclude that different diets can markedly influence the glycogen stores in the muscles. The ability to perform heavy, prolonged exercise is correspondingly affected and the higher the initial glycogen content the better the performance.... A group of subjects participated twice in a 30-km race, cross-country running, on the first occasion after their normal mixed diet, and on the second occasion after a few days on an extremely rich carbohydrate diet after previously emptying the glycogen depots. At several points of the track the running time was recorded. It was calculated that the rate of glycogen utilization was 0.8 to 1.0 g/100 g muscle/hr.

Two conclusions can be drawn from this study: (1) a high glycogen content in the muscles did not enable the subject to attain a higher speed at the beginning of the race compared to the case when the initial glycogen level was low; (2) when the glycogen concentration approached zero, the speed was reduced. The lower the initial store the sooner this impairment in running occurred.

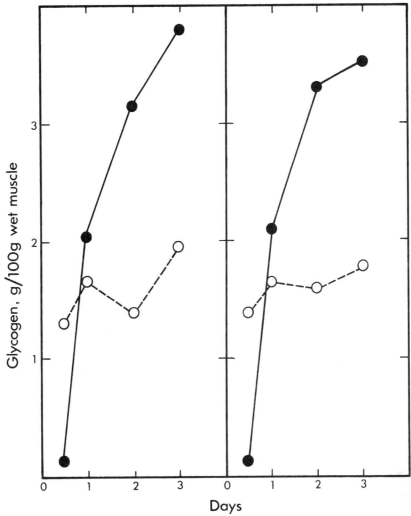

FIGURE 76 Two subjects were exercising on the same bicycle ergometer, one on each side, working with one leg while the other leg was resting (dashed line). After working to exhaustion, the subjects' glycogen content was analyzed in specimens from the lateral portions of the quadricipital muscle. Thereafter a carbohydrate-rich diet was followed for three days. Note that the glycogen content increased markedly in the leg that had been previously emptied of its glycogen content. (Illustration by courtesy of Textbook of Work Physiology.)

It should be pointed out that there is one drawback with the high glycogen storage: it was mentioned that each gram of glycogen is stored together with about 2.7 g of water. With a glycogen storage of 700 g there is therefore an increase in body water amounting to about 2 kg. In activities in which the body weight has to be lifted an excessive glycogen store should therefore be avoided.

After prolonged heavy exercise a maxi-

mal effort does not produce the same high blood lactic acid concentration as is normally found in connection with short-term exercise (Figure 77). This cannot be explained simply by emptied glycogen stores; there is, for some other reason, a gradual decrease in the capacity of the muscle cells to produce a tension high enough to initiate the anaerobic processes to maximal power. . . .

If glucose is infused continuously during

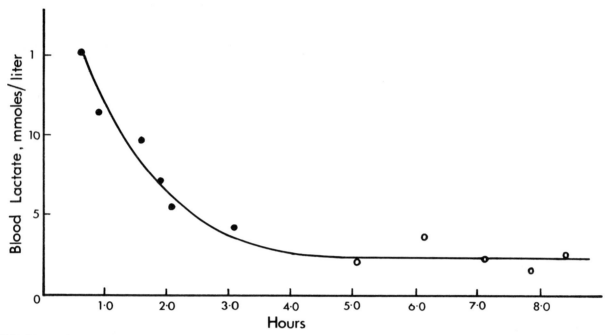

FIGURE 77   Concentration of blood lactic acid after competition of cross-country skiing of various durations, distance from 10–85 km. Solid dots represent mean values, circles represent individual values. (Illustration by courtesy of Textbook of Work Physiology.)

exercise, bringing the blood sugar level well above 200 mg/100 ml blood, the fall in muscle glycogen is significantly smaller than under normal conditions. . . . The difference in this reduction is, however, not large. It seems as if glucose administered during exercise will to some extent replace the utilization of free fatty acids. . . .

The beneficial effect of the sugar supply may be more pronounced when the glycogen depots are depleted. Various factors may then facilitate the transport of glucose across the cell membrane of the muscle cell.

The glycogen content of the liver is 50 to 100 g. This acts as the carbohydrate store to maintain the blood glucose level and indirectly to supply glucose to the nervous tissue which has no carbohydrate reserve of its own.

Summary   The ability to perform heavy prolonged exercise is directly related to the initial glycogen stores of the

working muscle. From about 1.5 g/100 g muscle after a mixed diet the glycogen content may, after about 2 hrs. of work with 75 percent of the maximal oxygen uptake, approach zero, and the subject becomes exhausted.

It is possible to increase the glycogen content of the muscles by a carbohydrate-rich diet (to about 2.5 g/100 g muscle). The effect will be still more pronounced if prolonged exercise to exhaustion precedes this special diet (up to 4 g/100 g muscle). Even higher values (up go 5 g/100 g muscle) can be obtained if the low glycogen content of the muscle is maintained low for a few days by eating fat and proetin wtih no carbohydrates included in the diet. . . . [7]

I have been at pains to demonstrate the effects a hard game will have upon the body. You cannot avoid the build-up of heat; nor the sweating; nor the depletion of glycogen from the muscles, but you can slow the processes through training and diet.

What is happening to you is also happening to your opponent, so make him work a little harder and so use his reserves at a faster rate.

RECOMMENDED TRAINING PROGRAM

Over many years as coach and player I have developed a training regimen which has proved to be highly successful for me and my pupils. It is designed to give suppleness combined wtih muscle and body tone.

Being a squash player and not a wrestler, my requirement is for muscles to perform efficiently on command, so my weight training is done with two 10 lb. dumb-bell weights. It is preferable to use light weights, and many repetitions of the one exercise, than working with heavy weights. For preference I work out in the morning before breakfast, but there is neither advantage nor disadvantage in selecting any other time so long as one trains regularly.

Exercise Sequence

I start by doing a number of bending exercises which stretch and loosen the muscles, then continue with those for shoulders, back and abdomen. (See Figure 78.)

Exercise 1 Stand with legs apart, hands interlocked above the head, with right palm facing right and left palm to the left. Touch the outside of the left foot (knees stiff), touch the floor between the feet, push down once; touch outside right foot, then stretch back to original position, keeping arms stiff. Repeat twenty times, then twenty times starting from the right side.

Exercise 2 Push-ups. Lie flat on the floor, hands as wide apart as the shoulders, fingers slightly spread and straight ahead. Push up to the full stretch of the arms, ensuring that the body is kept straight. Slowly lower the body to the floor. Repeat forty times.

Exercise 3 Lie on the stomach with clasped hands stretched in front of the body, feet together. Raise the hands and legs (stiff) simultaneously as high as possible, pause, and lower. Repeat fifty times.

Exercise 4 Lie on the back, feet together, legs stretched in front of the body, hands clasped behind the head. Sit up and at the same time draw the legs up keeping the feet off the floor. Touch the outside of the left knee with the right elbow then return to prone position. Sit up once again touching the right knee with the left elbow. Repeat fifty times.

Thigh Muscles

Fifty knee bends follow but here I must issue a word of warning. Studies have shown that great harm can be done to the knee joint if: (a) the body is allowed to go down as far as possible, and/or (b) the bend is made with weights. The knee joint is a delicate, complicated mechanism that can be strained more readily than is generally appreciated, but exercised correctly it can be strengthened so as to operate with greater efficiency and be less liable to damage.

To develop and maintain the strength and endurance of the quadriceps, a half knee bend is recommended, just deep enough for the thighs to be parallel with the floor.

Ankle Strengthening

The rapid changes of direction which occur during a game place high demands on the ankles, so these need strength and flexibility. Three simple exercises provide the requirements:

Exercise 1 Stand next to a doorway, wall, or anything that enables you to maintain balance, heels together, toes pointed out. Come up on the toes to full stretch, then lower the heels. Repeat thirty times.

Exercise 2 Same position but this time raise the toes to the full limit. Lower toes to the floor. Repeat thirty times.

109

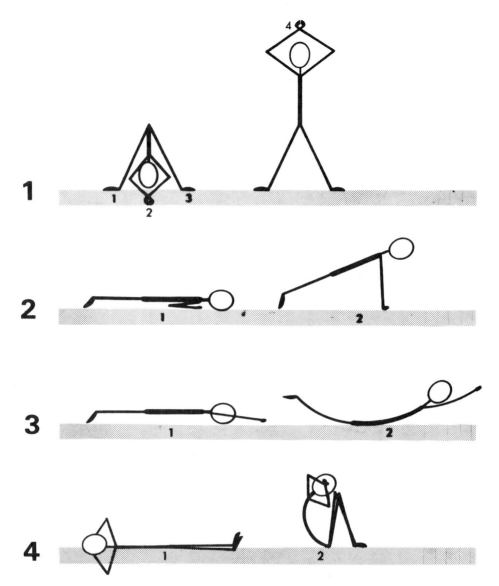

FIGURE 78   Basic exercise program designed to tone the muscles.

Exercise 3   Toes together, heels apart; come up on the toes to the full stretch. Lower the heels to the floor. Repeat thirty times.

Weight Training

Exercise 1   Hold a dumb-bell weight in each hand, arms stretched fully in front of the body. Keeping the arms stiff, bring back as far as possible with the hands remaining at shoulder height. Return arms to the front of the body. Repeat twenty times.

Exercise 2   Hold a weight in each hand with the arms beside the body. Raise both forearms fully, keeping the upper part of the arms in the vertical position. Slowly lower the arms. Repeat one-hundred times.

Exercise 3   Start with the weights held beside the shoulders. Extend the arms fully upwards, returning to the shoulders. Repeat fifty times.

Exercise 4   Lock the fingers around one weight, hold above the head with arms extended, feet apart. Keeping the arms stiff, bend fully to the left and then to the right. Repeat twenty times.

Road Training

The muscles have now been warmed up, which guards against strain occurring during road training. I run three miles along a defined stretch of road which takes me 1½ miles from home. This ensures that if I am ever tempted to stop, I am faced with the distance back, so I consider that I might as well run back as walk. The temptation is always present to shorten the distance if one runs around an oval. A brisk cold shower upon returning home, then breakfast. There are times when a run is not possible because of weather but this can be replaced by running on the spot, inside the house, for fifteen or twenty minutes. Make sure that effectiveness is obtained by raising the knees to a fairly high position on each step.

Equipment

To carry out a training program similar to the one above, your only investment is in a pair of dumb-bell weights, but the return on that investment is good health and stamina on the squash court.

Diet

Over recent years a great deal of publicity has been given to the high levels of cholesterol in animal fats. There may or may not be truth in the claims (I am not qualified to judge), but if the claims are true I believe that the person who exercises regularly, and with sufficient exertion, will never have a cholesterol build-up in the bloodstream.

I do not advocate any special diet; just maintain a balanced diet, eating with commonsense, except when anticipating a hard match, and then follow the rich carbohydrate plan mentioned earlier. The one concession I do make however, is the daily supplement of one multivitamin and one 500 mg vitamin C tablet.

The Caloric Cost of Running But if you are overweight and want to reduce . . . a new study by a research team from the Air Force Academy in Colorado shows the exact caloric consumption involved in running approximately 1.45 miles, depending on the weight of the runner and the speed with which he runs.

According to the study, a 170 pound man running the distance in 8 minutes would burn up 175 calories. Running more slowly—16 minutes for the 1.45 miles—he would use 157 calories. A 120-pounder would expend fewer calories for the same exercise output; a 220-pounder would burn considerably more.

One finding of the study is that the speedster tho tears up the track burns only a few more calories than the jogger who putters along at an easy pace. In the case of the 170-pounder, he used only 18 fewer calories at slow speed. But for purposes of fitness, say the researchers, the faster running speed is much better for toning up heart and lung action than in leisurely trotting.

Of course, an expenditure of 3,500 calories still is necessary to burn one pound of fat, and exercise can't do it alone. But if an expenditure of only 100 calories is maintained daily through exercise, there would be a 10 pound weight loss in a year, the researchers point out.

The accompanying chart, will permit you to figure out how much weight you can lose by running 1.45 miles per day at varying rates of speed, according to your own present weight. [8]

Caloric values for running 2.413 km (1.45 mi.)									
Weight		Calories/min							
kg	(lbs.)	8	9	10	11	12	13	14	15	16
54.5	(120)	125	124	121	120	119	117	116	114	112
59.0	(130)	135	133	132	130	128	126	125	123	121
63.6	(140)	145	143	141	139	138	136	134	132	130
68.1	(150)	155	153	151	149	147	145	143	141	139
72.6	(160)	165	163	161	159	156	154	152	150	148
77.2	(170)	175	173	170	168	166	164	161	159	157
81.7	(180)	185	182	180	178	175	173	171	168	166
86.3	(190)	195	192	190	187	185	182	180	177	175
90.8	(200)	205	202	199	197	194	192	189	186	184
95.3	(210)	215	212	209	206	204	201	198	195	193
99.9	(220)	225	222	219	216	213	210	207	204	202

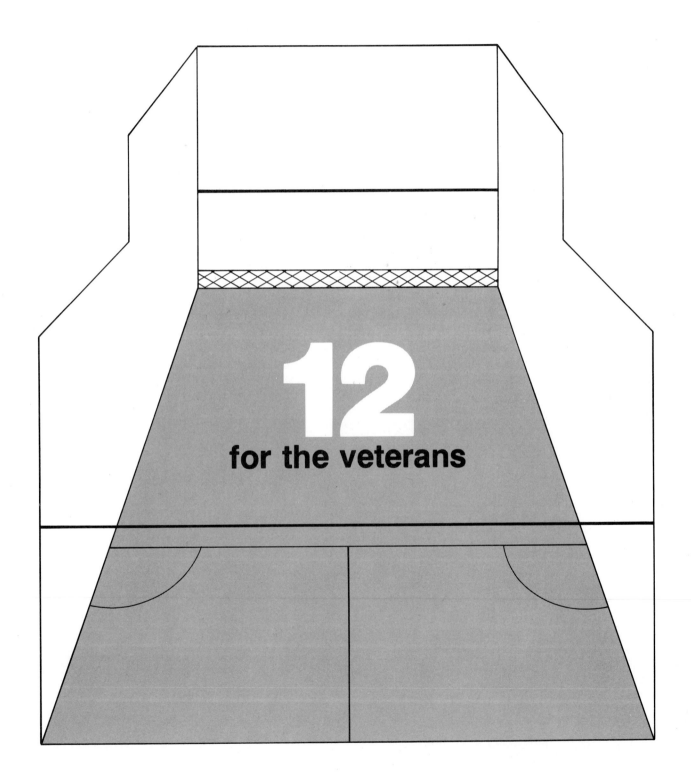

WHO IS A VETERAN?

I dislike the use of the term *veteran* to describe the more mature player of the game as, for me, it has connotations of the geriatic. However, it has become a word in common usage so I am prepared to go along and continue to use it rather than try to introduce any other name.

The most generally recognized cut-off age is forty-five, which seems as good a period as any in one's life to be called a veteran and become eligible to enter into selected tournaments. Nevertheless, I know of many players of this maturity, and greater, who can outrun and outplay most men ten or even fifteen years younger. Veterans clubs are springing up in all the major squash-playing countries with the object of helping to create or expand the facilities for those players who wish to not only continue to play the game but to compete against members of similar age.

The veteran at club or championship level is the player who has played the game for many years; he is *not* one who, in mature years decides to take up the game for the first time. Squash can be played from an early age through to advanced years, but it is downright foolish to think that one can commence playing such an active game later in life if the body has not been conditioned early on, and if one has not played both continuously and regularly.

HOW OLD *IS* A MAN OF FORTY-FIVE?

Biologically there is nothing we can do about aging, and it is a fact that tomorrow we will be a day older than we are today. Reflexes will be slower, muscles less responsive, aerobic capacity reduced, sight lengthened, etc.—these are all part of the process of growing old. But if one has carried out over the years, and continued to follow, a well-designed training program, biological age can be effectively reduced by ten to fifteen years.

The fitness training program described in Chapter 11 is designed for just this purpose, to assist squash players of any age and standard. However, for the veteran of forty-five, it effectively brings his biological age back to that comparable with a man of thirty-five or thirty years old. It must not be construed from this statement that one will live an additional ten or fifteen years. Certainly not, but the span of *squash-playing years* can be extended. I know a number of men in their sixties and seventies who play regularly, but squash has been their sport all their lives, and with advancing years they have adjusted to the slower body mobility and reflexes, by adopting changes in style. In addition, they are not foolish enough to think of going on to the court for a strong work-out with a teenager. Nevertheless they still enjoy the game to the full, gaining physical exercise and mental stimulation.

For the average veteran, the type of game which is obviously most suitable is one where skill predominates over stamina and mobility; where it is not too difficult to make a winning stroke such that an opponent's loose or weak return can be attacked; and the rallies are kept to a tolerably short duration. These senior players find long rallies exhausting, especially the exertion of going up-court for the short ball, back again to the T, or to the back corner to retrieve the well-directed lob.

The needs of the veteran vary from those of the younger, more mobile man, and proposals have been made to alter the rules to benefit veteran squash play. In recognition of the plain fact that veterans, being slower and sometimes even ponderous in their movements, cannot get out of each other's way to the extent that is desirable, and is, in fact, envisaged in the present rules, consideration could be given to altering the rules governing lets and penalty points, to allow for greater flexibility in interpretation. However, if one is to judge purely from watching play in veterans championships, it is obvious that some veterans are well able to hold their own in competitive squash against younger men in the main amateur championships. So it is doubtful if much will be gained through change or alteration of the rules. Apart from a preference for play on a slow court, with a slow ball, it must be left to the veteran to adapt his game to cope with advancing years.

CHOICE OF OPPONENT

Squash is always more enjoyable to both watch and play when the contestants are of much the same ability. This is particularly true of the veteran's game, where differences in, and reduced, mobility can be quite pronounced. Undoubtedly, for obvious reasons, those in the veteran class prefer opponents from around their own age group. The veteran with greater skill and experience may well be able to exert these attributes to beat a younger man who may feel, at the end of the game, that he has not had a proper run and be left with the feeling of having been tricked rather than beaten. On the other hand, there is the skilful, younger player who has the speed to counter the veteran's best strokes, leaving him with a sense of frustration, and creating the distinct possibility of him overstraining himself in an effort to keep the game going, and/or prove his prowess.

The after-the-game session is more a part of the veteran's squash than that of his younger opponent, and this builds up a rapport which should always be part of the game. Another reason why, as far as possible, *like should play with like.*

COMPETITIONS FOR OTHER AGE GROUPS

The arbitrary age of forty-five, which determines when a player is considered a veteran, is as good a starting point as any, for we must have some benchmark against which to measure performance. But having set this milestone in a player's life where he graduates to the senior ranks, one can see no reason why championships cannot be held for those who have passed through other birth dates.

TACTICS FOR THE VETERAN

The Psychological Advantage

An important aspect that should not be overlooked is that although the body may age, and for want of a better word, deteriorate, the brain does not, being capable of continuing to accept and store knowledge and information. For the veteran, the psychological advantage that he may have over an opponent can be of tremendous importance.

When watching top-class players, one is at first astounded by the retrieving, and positively staggered by the speed and anticipation they demonstrate. Then having accepted this standard of play as normal (and not always fully appreciating the tactics being employed), spectators can be excused for getting bored when rallies seem to be of never-ending duration, with the ball continuing to be played up and down the wall to a length as a drive or lob. The accent in this class of squash is on defense, and in the percentage game, on letting the opponent make the mistakes. Each knows that the other possesses the skills to retrieve virtually anything and hit a winner from the loose ball. To go for a killing shot at the wrong time would be too risky and could turn the tide during the match. But how much more enjoyable it is for spectators to watch two good veterans match skills and tactics, and it is, I am sure, in many respects a more enjoyable game to play.

The beginners among my pupils are instructed from the start of their lessons that it is all-important to learn first to control the ball and not try to emulate the top level of players who play the power game, and can retrieve and run interminably. Nevertheless, they are encouraged to watch the champions in action, to study their game and, hopefully, learn.

Power versus Touch

However, they are also obliged to watch and study the veterans as a means of comparing the power game with that of the touch tactician—the veteran—for whom sheer accuracy is even more important to deny the opponent easy balls from which he may attempt winners.

The veteran's game requires a great measure of thought and analysis of the situation at hand, for he must compensate for the loss of speed and mobility by attempting to anticipate that split-second earlier, and by employing the *touch* that he has developed over the years, to play more drop shots and angles, which are more likely to be winners because of his accuracy.

Playing the Delayed Shot

In order to bustle an opponent continually and deny him time to get set for a shot, I advocate, as a general rule, taking the ball as early as possible. But for the veteran there is every reason for him to delay the shot, hitting it late rather than early. The game for the veteran must undergo changes in tactics to accommodate his advancing years, reduced mobility and speed, slower reflexes and muscular reaction, and purely and simply, his running out of wind.

It is not a matter of going to bed one night at the age of forty-four, waking-up next morning aged forty-five, and changing one's game completely. The change is psychological, gradual, and one of development over the years in a player's career. The thinking player will appreciate what is happening to his fitness and will adjust his game accordingly, to become with wily *touch* exponent, as opposed to his younger club members—the fitness fanatics, who chase and retrieve continuously.

Service—
the Veteran's Trump Card

When I first played Hashim Khan I asked him what he tried to achieve with his service, to which he replied that he was merely getting the ball into play and so commence the rally, and that, while he wasn't too interested in where it went, on the other hand he didn't want to make it too easy for his opponent to return.

All well and good if you are Hashim! But there will never be another player as good, so my advice to pupils of any age or standard of play is to concentrate on the service, presenting your opponent with as difficult a ball and as big a problem as possible. For the veteran, the service is the most important shot of all, the start of the rally when he holds every advantage. He should not throw this advantage to the wind and be like so many players, young as well as senior, who amble into the box, casually hit the ball onto the front wall while still walking, hoping that it lands in the opponent's court, and having done this, take a leisurely stroll to the T.

Make the service an attacking shot, and above all *think*, take your time, and be in no hurry to serve. Be deliberate in what you do—correct stance, be balanced, pick the best aiming point on the front wall, and decide what type of service you want to deliver.

Lob to Win

For the veteran, the lob service is a must, to be used at all times, with the occasional hard or sliced varieties thrown in as surprise elements. Played with accuracy, the lob can be such that an opponent fails to make a return, mishits, or is forced into a back-corner defensive boast. But whatever, that good service has saved the player from any undue running on legs that will appreciate the reduced work load.

On occasions, the veteran will find himself playing on a court with a very low roof and be forced to alter his service from lob to one that is defensive, as a lob in these conditions would run the risk of hitting the roof. Other factors which would influence the use of a defensive service would be: if it were played on a fast court, with a fast ball, or against an opponent capable of playing the lob for winners into the corners. But all that apart, if the reader uses the service action advocated in Chapter 7, there will be no need to change style and attitude to cope with a low roof. I have never encountered any problem with the low roof when serving. An exponent, and proponent of taking the ball early when playing at any level or standard of squash, I nevertheless believe that for the veteran the delayed stroke has a number of advantages. My theories are not directed at the top few veterans competing at championship level, but more to the great number of players below this standard who may not possess the physical and technical attributes of their more compe-

tent compatriots. Top-class veterans are able to win rallies against younger players, but when competing against men of comparable age are able to play winners with certainty and regularity from balls presented to them in the front half of the court. This ability comes naturally from skill and experience but is also partly attributable to delaying the shot and playing it late.

The Advantages of a Slow Ball

Irrespective of whether played in the tropics or in a colder climate, top-level championship play results in the ball getting quite hot, making the *touch* shot somewhat difficult and in any case, risky, as players of this caliber are fast around the court, can retrieve, and possess the full repertoire of strokes. Not so for the veteran who, while still capable of playing a range of shots, may not have the power to raise the temperature of the ball to such a degree, and in fact should be happier playing with a slower-moving ball. For him the slower ball bestows an advantage, allowing for *touch*, for stroke play which involves fewer risks, and having sufficient speed to respond to the wishes of the striker.

Recognition of One's Physical Limitations

The veteran should be conscious of his physical limitations, relating them to his opponent, and be mindful that while he may not have the stamina, speed, and mobility of his earlier years, neither has his opponent. If it is accepted that the odds are tipped in favor of the delayed stroke, under no circumstances should the taking of the early ball be discarded completely. The basics of the game remain. It is only the tactics, application, and mental and physical approach which alter to accommodate the changing circumstances.

Immobilize the Opponent

The game is played at a slower pace— ball, players, stroking—and the whole tempo allows more time for thought, and to plan the shot in hand as well as those in the future. In playing the delayed ball, the veteran has in effect allowed his opponent to get into position for the anticipated return. But if this is a disadvantage when playing a younger, fitter, or more mobile person, the veteran opponent may not react fast enough, be immobilized for that split second and so be caught on the wrong foot through slower reflex action.

By delaying the stroke the veteran has allowed his opponent to commit himself to replying to a certain shot and has in effect restricted his own movements so catching himself wrong-footed. As he enters the ranks of the seniors, the veteran will come equipped with a range of shots he has acquired and developed over the years, and be quite capable of playing any one of them from a given favorable position if not under pressure. The inability to run and retrieve as he did when he was younger demands that he allow himself time to get into position and play the shot of his choice without rush or bustle.

The Need for More Frequent Winners

Speed and mobility certainly suffer with increasing age, but more so does stamina which, tending to lag behind speed during the teenage years, seems to fade faster still in later life. Evidence of this comes from the fact that long-distance and marathon runners come from a somewhat more mature group, whereas sprints are dominated by the younger brigade. Lacking both speed and stamina, the veteran no longer has the resources to make continuous sorties up to the front for a drop shot, and then run back to the corners for a well-directed lob. Not for him the luxury of the percentage game, playing safe and allowing his opponent to make all the mistakes. He cannot afford to be as patient as he was ten or fifteen years earlier when his energy store and stamina were greater.

Certainly on occasions take the early ball and venture up front to retrieve the short boast or drop shot, but be careful to pace yourself and not over-extend what physical resources you have too early in the game. Use these tactics sparingly, a few rallies at a time, and assess the effect it is having on the opponent. If you can anticipate the opponent's return, this presents an excellent opportunity for taking an early ball; for example a good service by you, which forces a boast and enables you to play a drop shot counter. The opponent's reduced mobility, like yours, allows the quickly taken ball by you, to be played for a winner more often against another veteran.

Long Rallies Are Dangerous

The veteran cannot allow long rallies to develop, and is forced to play for winners more often than would otherwise be recommended. But it is even more essential that when the *killing shot* is tried it is a winner, for the poor shot enables the opponent to get up and try a winner himself. Never allow the opponent the luxury of playing from the front of the court. Keep him back and take command of the T by accurate lobbing and drives to a length.

SUMMARY

To summarize, the veteran's game should center around:

- a good lob service

- drives down the wall to a length

- accurate lobs to the back corners, forcing from this and the drives a boasted return

- playing the delayed ball more often than the early one

- "masking" the shot with the body, keeping the ball from the opponent's view

- going for the killing shot more often, but making sure it is a winner

- command of the T

- keeping the opponent from the front half of the court

- knowing your level of fitness and stamina, and pacing yourself accordingly

- avoiding getting into long rallies.

119

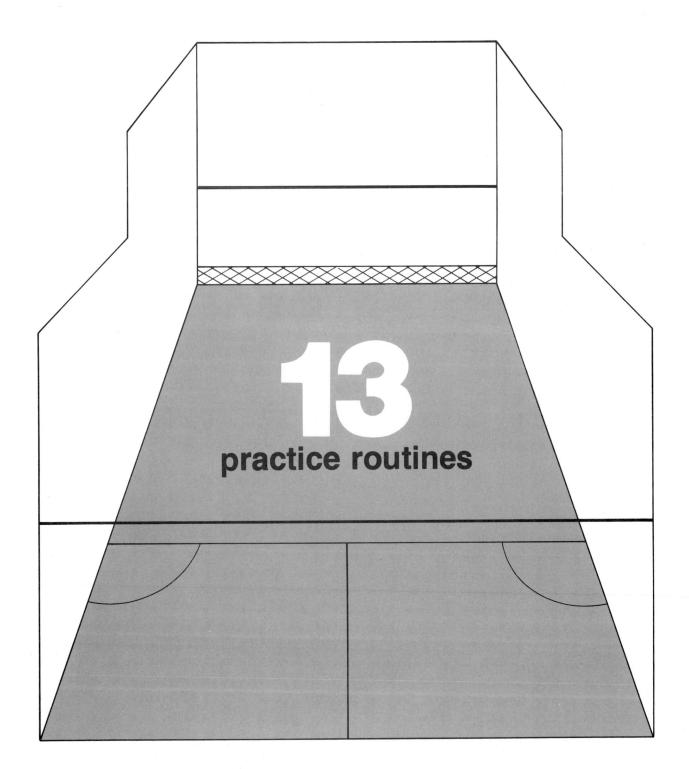

13
practice routines

INTRODUCTION

Proficiency in the game can only come as a result of practice, both with and without an opponent. In an earlier chapter the reader was advised to play with both better and weaker opponents as a means of improving his game. It is now proposed to analyze what can be done when one is alone. It is appreciated that one does not always have time, or the availability of a court, to allow individual practice, but if one is to improve and reach the top, this is an essential requirement of the game.

PREREQUISITES

Practicing alone can be boring, requiring dedication, but let us not discount the benefits which accrue if one is prepared to extend the effort. Practice makes perfect, so the saying goes, but unless correctness is the keynote of the practice it can produce negative results by reinforcing errors.

First seek the advice of a good coach so that you know what you are, and should be doing. His advice is invaluable, representing money well spent. And you need a return on the investment of time devoted to practice, so to maximize this return, analyze every shot you make, be it good or bad. Was the ball too far from the wall? Could I have hit it harder or softer, higher or lower for a length? Why did that boast hit the tin? How can I get the lob service into the corner? Always *Why? How? Where?*

Ensure that there is method in your practice rather than just hitting the ball all over the court. That is wasted effort. Go onto the court with a plan in your mind of what you want to do. Maybe the backhand down the wall is giving you some problem; if so, practice this shot, not once or twice, but until you feel happy about the stroke. Then go on to another aspect of your game.

Devote time to the serve. You hold every advantage when serving, so aim to make it as difficult as possible for your opponent. Practice the lob, watching where the ball lands in relation to where it was hit on the front wall, and at what speed. Play the fast serve and the slice, once again analyzing the ball travel and court landing-position.

PRACTICE ROUTINES

It is recommended that players, in addition to practicing all shots, undertake the following helpful routines which I have devised. They were designed more for developing and improving ball control than anything else, but isn't ball control what the game is all about?

Practice 1 Stand at the T. Play a forehand to the left front wall, just above the tin and one foot from the side wall. The ball will rebound to the T, enabling you to play a backhand to the right front wall. With practice you will be able to, and should, adjust the stroking to hit harder or softer, higher and further from the side wall so that the ball always rebounds to the T. (See Figure 79.)

Practice 2 Once again stand at the T. Play a backhand to the right front wall in the form of a drop shot, but hard enough to rebound some distance. Having played the shot, move forward so that the next is played closer to the corner, and slower. Repeat, continuing to advance until you are near the corner, playing to the same wall position. Figure 80 shows the movement from A to B. Once at position B, back-track to the T. Once ball control has been achieved on the backhand, practice the forehand.

Not only does this practice routine help ball control, it also establishes confidence and the ability in playing the drop shot.

It being essential that the correct stance be taken up before hitting the ball (left foot across the forehand, right foot for the backhand), coaches should ensure that this action becomes completely instinctive. I have found the routine described below to be most useful in instilling this action in beginners.

Practice 3 The pupil, in the confines of his bedroom, with no one watching, stands in front of the mirror and does what can best be described as a small dance step. Face the mirror, feet apart, then rising up on the toes, put the left foot across to the right, take a short simulated swing at an imaginary ball (no racket required), then swing across to the left in a 1–2–3, 1–2–3, skipping action. Practiced every day, this routine quickly builds up the correct action on the court.

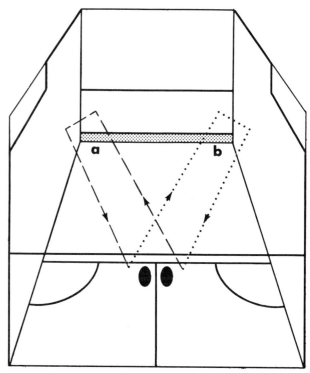

FIGURE 79 Practice routine designed to achieve ball control.

FIGURE 80 Practice routine designed to perfect the drop shot. Show for the forehand. Reverse the action to practice the backhand.

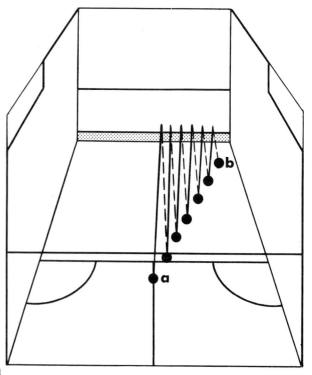

124

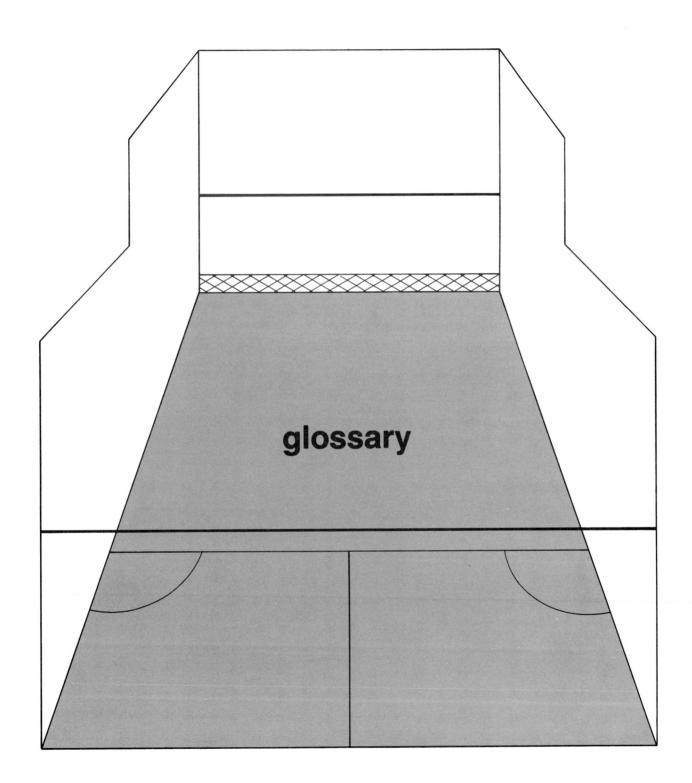

glossary

Board The expression denoting a band, the top edge of which is 17 inches from the floor across the lower part of the front wall, above which the ball must be returned before the stroke is good.

Cut Line A line set out upon the front wall, the top edge of which is 6.6 feet above the floor, and extending the full width of the court. (N.B.: All the lines in the court should be red.)

Fault A service that strikes the front wall between the tin and the cut line; or lands short of the short line; or lands in the server's court.

Game and Match Ball The state of the game when the server requires one point to win is said to be game ball.

Half-court Line A line set out upon the floor, parallel to the side walls, dividing the back half of the court into two equal parts.

Length The ball that strikes the back-wall nick on the second bounce.

Let In general terms, the recommencement of the rally with the same server. The rules on let are quite lengthy and players are advised to obtain a copy of these rules.

Nick The corner where the floor meets the wall.

Not-up The expression used to denote that a ball has not been served or returned above the board in accordance with the rules.

Out The ball is out when it touches the front, sides, or back of the court above the area prepared for play or passes over any cross bars or other part of the roof of the court. The lines delineating such area, the lighting equipment, and the roof are out.

Service Box, or Box A delineated area in each half court from within hand-in serves.

Short Line   A line set out upon the floor, parallel to and 22 feet from the front wall, and extending the full width of the court.

Striker   The player whose turn it is to play after the ball has hit the front wall.

Stop   Expression used by the referee to stop play.

Tin   A strip of resonant material covering the lower part of the front wall between the board and the floor.